# SHMUEL'S BRIDGE

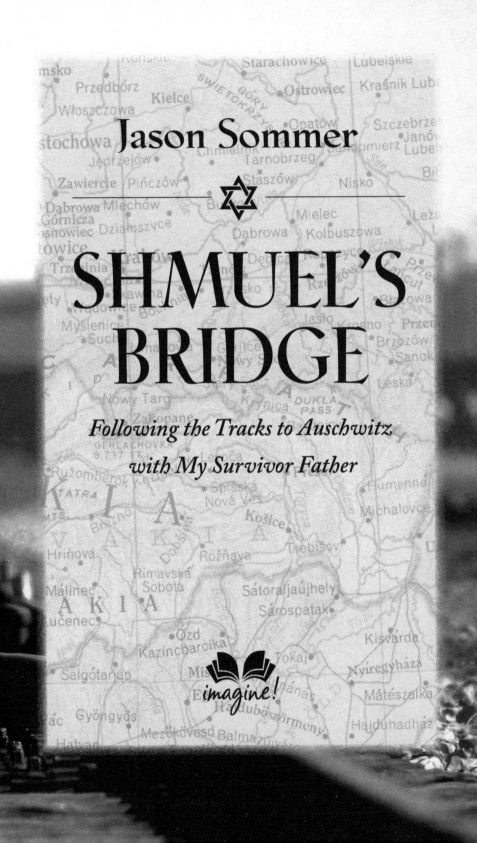

# Jason Sommer

✡

# SHMUEL'S BRIDGE

*Following the Tracks to Auschwitz*

*with My Survivor Father*

*imagine!*

An Imagine Book
Published by Charlesbridge
9 Galen Street
Watertown, MA 02472
(617) 926-0329
www.imaginebooks.net

**Library of Congress Cataloging-in-Publication Data**
Names: Sommer, Jason, author.
Title: Shmuel's bridge: following the tracks to Auschwitz
with my survivor father / Jason Sommer.
Description: Watertown, MA: Charlesbridge, [2022]. | Summary: "A memoir
recounting the author's trip with his survivor father to Eastern Europe
to locate the bridge where his uncle was killed on the way to
Auschwitz." —Provided by publisher.
Identifiers: LCCN 2020057810 (print) | LCCN 2020057811 (ebook) |
ISBN 9781623545123 (hardcover) | ISBN 9781632892393 (ebook)
Subjects: LCSH: Sommer, Jason—Family. | Sommer, Jason—Travel—Europe,
Eastern. | Auschwitz (Concentration camp) | Holocaust, Jewish
(1939–1945) | Children of Holocaust survivors—United States. | Fathers
and sons. | Jews—Identity. | Identity (Psychology)
Classification: LCC D804.196.S645 2022 (print) | LCC D804.196 (ebook) |
DDC 940.53/18 [B]—dc23
LC record available at https://lccn.loc.gov/2020057810
LC ebook record available at https://lccn.loc.gov/2020057811

Display type set in Phaistos
Text type set in Adobe Caslon Pro
Printed and bound by Berryville Graphics
Production supervision by Jennifer Most Delaney
Jacket and interior design by Lilian Rosenstreich

Printed in the United States of America
(hc) 10 9 8 7 6 5 4 3 2 1

All interior photographs are printed courtesy of the author, except for the photo on page 44, courtesy of Toshi Tasaki, and the photo on page 71, courtesy of the Ronald Reagan Presidential Library.

Map credits: Lionel Pincus and Princess Firyal Map Division, The New York Public Library. "Map of upper New York City and adjacent country: showing the city above 125th Street" The New York Public Library Digital Collections. 1890, Lionel Pincus and Princess Firyal Map Division, The New York Public Library. "Ohman's Standard Map of the Bronx." The New York Public Library Digital Collections. 1917, Lionel Pincus and Princess Firyal Map Division, The New York Public Library. "Map of the enlarged City of Brooklyn, published for the Brooklyn Directory" The New York Public Library Digital Collections. 1894, Lionel Pincus and Princess Firyal Map Division, The New York Public Library. "New and correct map of the Great Rock Island route, Chicago, Rock Island & Pacific Railway: the passengers favorite route between Chicago and Council Bluffs, Kansas City, Leavenworth, Atchison, Minneapolis, St. Paul and all points east, west, south-west, and north-west" The New York Public Library Digital Collections. 1883, "Bartholomew's chart of the world on Mercator's projection" by Norman B. Leventhal Map Center at the BPL is licensed under CC BY 2.0, Lionel Pincus and Princess Firyal Map Division, The New York Public Library. "Obuda, (Budapest)." The New York Public Library Digital Collections. 1910.

*for Meilech Steinberger*
*for Shmuel Steinberger*

— I I I I —

*Dem emess meg men zogen af dem eigenen taten.*
One may tell the truth about one's own father.
YIDDISH PROVERB

# Contents

# Preface

*he thought*
*he heard his father stir in the next room.*
*His father's sleep is delicate, forbidden*
*to disturb. He had been somewhere terrible*
*and narrowly come through....*

LIKE THIS PREFACE, each chapter in this book begins with lines from poems of mine, poems that testify to a long involvement in rendering the Holocaust stories of my family—my aunt, my uncle, and above all my father. (The sources of each excerpt can be found on page 205.) These poems have been meant to preserve not only what they retell—what has been told to me—but to say something about the telling itself, how such stories are transmitted and received, how lives form around survivors and their narratives. How my life did, anyway.

Much of my poetry has been an attempt to comply with the explicit charge made to me by survivors to write about what happened to them. But the poems have also been a chance to have my own voice heard among those whose experiences were more significant than my own, to try to make sense of what it is to come after. This book attempts a similar task. *Shmuel's Bridge* has its origin in my proximity, my love, for those whose lives were far more difficult than mine, made so by the obsession of Germans, Hungarians, and others to injure, to enslave, and then to murder them. Awareness of that dark fact, and the obligation that came with it, has never been far from my mind, even in childhood, before I could properly articulate it, or as a young adult, when I wanted to resist it.

This book represents an opportunity to examine the impact of the personal history of my father and his family more freely, more fully, perhaps, than poems allow. Central to that examination is a literal journey that my father and I took in Hungary, Poland, Slovakia, and the Ukraine, traveling to places that were the setting of his Holocaust experiences and that of others dear to him.

I did not set out on that journey with a book project in mind. Indeed, it took a very long time for that trip to become this book, and it would not have happened at all except for the encouragement and belief of one gifted novelist turned editor. Kevin Stevens, familiar with my poems, encouraged me to take on this memoir and served as the ablest of guides.

I also owe gratitude to others for their support, of which this book is only the latest example in a long reliance. I could not have hoped for better first responders. If I started out with the good fortune of having a wonderful writer for an editor, my readers were similarly a talented group of poets, teachers, and writers in various hyphenated combinations:

I thank Rich Moran for his most careful and detailed responses to the manuscript. Were that his only contribution it would have been sufficient, but hours of conversation helped me think through and shape what I was writing.

Historian and author David Marwell appears as himself in these pages, where I call him the source of all things historical—and so he has been, steering me to resources and being a resource himself as he answered my questions and shared his erudition with the utmost generosity.

Poet Alan Shapiro has been in this, as in years of my literary efforts, the wisest and best of advisers, always identifying the heart of the matter and helping me to get there.

Poet Chuck Sweetman assisted perhaps more than he knows—not only in applying his able mind and eye in reading the draft, but in his availability for thoughtful literary exchange all along the way.

Poet Jane Wayne, who thinks people go on too much in acknowledgments, must nevertheless be made aware of how I valued her reactions to early sections as well as the final draft.

My wife, Allison Brock, assumed more than her fair share of household duties so that I could do this work. A professional editor herself, she has made me better in these pages than I otherwise would have been—and made me better in my life.

Acknowledgments are also due to Harry and Lilly Muller, who gave of their stories and themselves over the years. Their memories have been a blessing. I have dedicated the book first to my father, by the name he had in boyhood and through the troubled time before America. Our travels together continue and I am thankful for them, especially because of the home place we have reached with one another.

NEW ROCHELLE, NEW YORK

# 1

*remembered, remembering.*
*Forgetting then, forgotten all*
*the passing things that anger was,*
*releasing one by one to silence*
*the words of several languages*

I OPEN THE BEDROOM DOOR SLOWLY.

"Dad, do you want to see the video?"

I edge in. My dad is resting on his side, hands palm to palm under his cheek, as if he has assumed a sleep pose rather than a sleep position. His eyes, less distinct than ever, are open but slow to track me as I move around the bed. His head is wintry, a scraggly tonsure of white hair around his mottled scalp, with a peppering of dark strands in the unruly eyebrows. Resting. In the double bed he looks diminished, less than his five foot eight. In his late nineties, he is thinner than he's ever been.

"See what?" he says.

He had gone into his room over an hour earlier to pray *maariv* and then apparently lay down to nap. His caregiver has reminded me it isn't a good idea to let him sleep too long during the day.

"Video," I repeat. "I have some video for you. You'll really like it."

I know he'll like it because he already has. In the past few days I have played selections from our 2001 trip over and over, and the pleasure he's shown I haven't seen from him in years. I feel guilty not to have managed it before—digitizing the videotapes, getting them onto memory sticks. Even as he got tired, welcoming my suggestion of a break, he would say, "Please, please, more later?"

"Video. Yes, video," he says flatly, deliberately a statement and not a question. I won't ask if he remembers what I showed him this morning. He bridles at any hint that anything is wrong, refuses to acknowledge any lapse. Refusal and denial got him through a war and a hard life before the war. He gets up and we leave the room.

"Our trip, you know, to Budapest and Munkacs?"

I have repeated this information many times over several days, as a casual aside, finessing by tone, as if it weren't obvious exposition. We sit at my laptop and I cue a clip not from the trip but just before it, a camera test I did on the eve our departure: a few minutes with my late mother and her cat. I have lost count of the number of times I have shown this to my dad, but each viewing is a surprise for him. And for me too, in a way. She's been gone seven years.

My mother on tape. Effusive. Alert. Conscious of the camera and of herself. And familiarly unreasonable with her pet, requiring the creature to sit still, elaborately interpreting her mewing, lavishing endearments on this ingrate who inevitably—I watch my dad as the moment approaches—whips round and swats her mistress. He smiles as the cat gets a mournful lecture on transgression. "Gigi," my mother says, "this was *no accident*." She clucks and scolds and informs Gigi at length that she doesn't measure up to Trooper, her deceased predecessor.

My father laughs exactly as he did the first time he saw this clip, and the many times since. "Look," he says. "Always the English teacher giving to the cat a lesson."

My family has a particular need to remember, a purpose in memory, and a particular vulnerability to forgetting. In the end, my mother knew only who we were, my father and I, and the end was more than ten years. But long before she was unable to make new memories, or to retrieve what had been there, she practiced making way for my father's, his need being greater. For his memories seared, and the embers might blaze at any time. They began in poverty around a place called, variously, in Hungarian, in

*Dad with his first love, Laura Launi, a medical student whom he met in the hospital while recovering from a life-threatening soccer injury*

Czech, in Ukrainian (depending on the shifting ownership), Munkacs, Mukacheve, Mukachevo. He still remembers those early days well, as he does his wartime youth as a forced laborer and escapee from the Nazis and his stint with the Russian army. Though now, at ninety-eight, his memories are under threat—an album of pictures that might be visible only one last time as they turn in the swirling tongues of a steady fire.

So I prompt him these days, as I shape my own memories of that 2001 trip, not only with the video I took then but with photographs of that journey and other pictures that reach back to long before I knew him. I want to see what he remembers and what it will cost him to. I want to see how he can help with the task I have put to myself, which concerns his memories and mine and what they have cost already, and how they might yet be of value.

A few weeks before I had the video ready to show him—the footage of our visit to his home village, to the site of his brother's murder, to Auschwitz—I decided to nudge him gently in that direction, as it were, by showing him photographs from a shoebox of prints I had fetched from his hall closet: a little heap of black-and-whites in assorted sizes, mostly loose; three yellow envelopes with uniform color sets, four by not-quite-six; and a scattering of negatives at the bottom. I also brought my tablet with a few things on it I wanted him to see.

He was at the table completing a second dinner. These days he sometimes forgets the first and eats again, a good thing since recent dental work has made chewing painful and he has been losing weight. I began with the black-and-white images, pre-America; there would be some pleasure for him in reviewing them. They were the easy ones. And of course he had seen them before.

The first was from his three years in a displaced persons camp in Italy, in Cremona, after the war. "You taught gymnastics there?" I asked him. Reminded him.

"And dance. Dance I taught, too. Ah, look at them, and me, all that hair."

A shock of dark hair, his widow's peak. These are the among the earliest pictures he has of himself, at twenty-one or -two, teaching refugee children, some of whom are only a head or so shorter than he.

Slipped in on the other side of that picture was one from slightly earlier: my dad on his motorcycle, the Jawa, from his time translating for his Russian liberators. The familiar gap between his teeth gave me a little start as I realized that the recent dental work had eliminated it.

It almost felt like a card trick as I randomly pulled out one photo after another. And he did respond, often, as if I had actually conjured something. He delighted at an action shot of himself on a soccer pitch, challenging another player for the ball, his leg extended in a deep lunge. He had played, I knew, with the team from the DP camp, where several teammates had been professional players before the war. He earned some money playing for them during his three years at the camp.

"You were a winger, right?" I said.

"Winger, either side. I can shoot with either foot."

I noted the present tense. A sort of fantasy.

"Still?"

"You want to play some tennis? Don't forget, you've never beaten me."

Palms out in mock protest, I said, "Hey, you have me over a barrel. I win, I've beaten a ninety-eight-year-old, and if I lose…well…"

He laughed.

I disliked my own awareness that I was priming him, but I wanted to work my way up to other places, to people he hadn't had to recognize for a long time, a few he had never identified for me. Curious as I was, I had never got around to asking, part of my dance of approach and avoidance over the years. And I was sure that for some of them it was too late. But there could be surprises too—sudden recoveries, unexpected sharpness. And this gallery would be a prelude to moving to the tablet, the computer, and in time the video.

Here was one he had spoken of before: a small snapshot with a thick white border of him standing with a girl under a tree. He hesitated, so I did what I sometimes do to nudge him, telling him a little of what he has told me before. It took him a moment, but his recollection stuttered back into fluency. She was his first love, Laura. She wasn't Jewish and history was against them: his surviving brother already had a sponsor for America, and my father was determined to follow him soon.

I had always been fascinated with the next one I slid from the pack: a woman in a fur hat gazing upward, lowered binoculars in her hand, a pistol at her waist. Years ago, when I came upon it first, he had said she was a

*Dad in action for the soccer team at the displaced persons camp in Cremona, after the war*

partisan but that was all. He claimed he didn't know her very well. Now not at all.

I pulled out one square of muted color from all the monochrome, a washed-out close-up of a woman on a blurred TV screen. My father had no response at all, and I was a little confused. I didn't even recognize the television set. And then it hit me: this was one of the many attempts my father had made to capture his mother's face, of which there is no image. Each time he tried, it might be a single feature he wanted to retrieve— broad cheekbones, the case this time, or else something about the eyes. This woman hadn't retained enough resemblance to jog his memory, or the photo was simply too faded. Still, he remained engaged and energetic, anticipating the next reveal.

I moved to color, fifty years on, to the envelopes that held scenes from his first return to his home region, in 1991. Just a few years before, the municipal government of Munkacs had forced the Jewish cemetery to move, his mother's grave with it. He and his brother had scrambled to find someone to ensure that my grandmother was reinterred properly and with a marker. The photograph I had in my hand, of the stone and my father standing by it, proved that they had succeeded. This was the record of the first time he was able to return without fear, or at all. The Soviets typically hadn't allowed visitors to the area, which had become part of the Ukraine, and there were cases of people who had been granted permission to visit and then were snatched by the authorities, on the grounds that they had been and were still citizens of the USSR. My father had had some reason to be afraid.

Many of these photographs were of his village, several miles southeast of Munkacs, called Kustanovice—his first school, his actual birthplace, or at least the grounds where his hut stood. Mostly they were places from the past, more durable than people, of course. Though there were some people—a childhood playmate, who looks ancient but was his age, and the daughter of a later Munkacs friend. He had traveled there with my mother on that 1991 trip, a decade before I was willing to go, or wanted to go, in fact. Several photos showed the two of them, little reprises as I thought of the sequence—the same scene: first with my father; then my father and her, between them a gravestone, like a trophy; again my father beside a plank door; and finally my father and her, on either side of the stone.

Ten years after this trip with my mother, I would go with him. Not just to his home village but to places with harsher memories: the labor camp in Budapest where he was enslaved; the roads and fields of Slovakia, where he had witnessed much atrocity and killing; Auschwitz, where most of his family perished; and the bridge, the fateful bridge in Poland.

It became my turn to go, to stand with him. Figuratively and actually. As I did weeks ago with the photographs, as I do now with the video, in mnemonic practice. My mother never had to prompt, only to be the most intent listener. Me, I am afraid not to prompt—afraid to let it all go. As if my efforts, or anyone's, were a guarantee. Still, the very thing about which I had so many reservations is what I must do now. Otherwise, I fear the part of his identity that often felt most at odds with mine will disappear, and soon. I will not know who he is then, and neither will he. And some part of myself, skeptical, defined in opposition, looking for a different and wider view of the events he speaks about—that will be gone, too. Without the resistance he has occasioned, I might suddenly push into an empty space. And there are others as well that I feel I will put in danger of vanishing into that emptiness. I think of one man in particular, a boy really, whom

*Dad in the middle of his first class of students: the survivor children at the DP camp in Cremona, where he taught ballroom dancing and gymnastics*

I never met, of whom I only have the vaguest picture. My uncle. I may be the only image that is left of him, a partial one at that. My father often said his kid brother was like me—I was like him, rather—tall like him, looked like him. Even my manner sometimes, he would remark, was so like his brother's, though how could that be?

I took another packet from the shoebox, labeled "Budapest" in my mother's precise hand. My father reached for it, but I asked him to wait, to put it by for another time. I opened my tablet.

I selected first an internet capture of a bridge, a railway bridge over a river. My father looked at it, then at me. "Do you recognize it?" I asked him.

He leaned in toward the screen and looked hard but gave no sign. I called up another picture I had found online, or rather two identical sepia photographs joined side by side for a stereopticon viewer.

"What do you think? The same bridge. From 1919. The Germans are rebuilding it after destroying it in the First World War. I have the caption in another file."

He could only tell me that the bridges were alike. And that was a beginning—it wouldn't require him admitting that he didn't remember, which he avoided saying. I wanted him to come along with me. I was trying to bring him slowly. One last image, not 1919 and not 1991. Again the bridge, the same one, but standing near the rails on some checker plate, with the crisscross of steel behind him, is my father.

"Poland," I said to him, "We were there together in 2001. I am behind the camera. That's my shadow on the ground."

My father moves into the kitchen, takes some grapes from the bowl, and looks at me. "So, are you going out?"

"No, Dad, I thought we'd have a look at the video, on the computer—we left off around Munkacs."

"OK. *Poshli, poshli,*" he says as he walks over to the small table by the door, crowded with equipment, screen and tower and printer. I seat him and take up the mouse. I have begun skipping certain scenes in the replays: the bridge we searched for and found, the brickyard where his family was put on the train, the footage I took in Auschwitz.

The video resumes in Kustanovice, his home village. He is unsure sometimes of what exactly he is looking at.

"This is outside your village," I say. "That's an old man who knew your father. That's me and you and Eva Kelenye."

"Oh, you know so well. I am glad you take such an interest."

He lights up with joy as he recognizes the view from the site of the hut in which he was born. In the blue distance are the foothills of the Carpathians. He turns to me and says, as he said earlier today, and yesterday, "This is a precious treasure; you must give me a copy."

"This *is* your copy, Dad, it's on your machine, there, right on the desktop—and everyone will be able to play it."

We view the tapes for a half hour or so and I notice him shifting in the chair, so I stop and say we can look at more later.

"Yes, please, later."

He gets up, drifts into the kitchen, has a little cornbread and milk. He goes back to his room, to the bathroom, comes back and asks several times about the schedule for synagogue services. Then he sits down at the dining room table and cries. He only shakes his head when I ask him why.

THE BRONX

# 2

*the dim light of the shoes*
*in pyramid, of the hair and clothes in bales,*
*the glitter of granary heaps of eyeglasses,*
*watches, jewelry.*

WHEN I WAS FIVE YEARS OLD, I had a bad dream and came looking for my mother for comfort, from the dark of my bedroom to the darkened living room, where, as I entered, her face was illuminated suddenly, as if swept by a searchlight. But the glare was only the white of a black-and-white film on television, a shot that had more sky than earth, an angle up through the wire to the watchtowers, with the wrought-iron inscription *Arbeit Macht Frei* arching above.

In that flash of light, my dream fear vanished in new alarm at finding my mother's face streaming tears. Another flare, and I turned again to the screen to see what she was seeing—a gleam of flesh, just for an instant, entrenched and shining out of a pit in the ground. Then shoes, a pyramid of shoes, like those I might see anyone wearing now but mixed with old-fashioned shoes with buttons and weathered work boots and a small sandal, a child's, near the top, its mate buried somewhere in that strange mound. The film was old, and its coarse grain seemed to catch and fling particles as dust leapt back and forth and a hair was snagged in frame, quivering, then whisked away.

Something kept me from speaking—mesmerized by the way the light on my mother's face kept changing, her tears glinting and then gone in the varying depths of shadow. I felt something else too, despite the lingering fear—the power she bestowed on me by not seeing me. Invisible, I watched with her as the film's gray blur and blackout turned to shoulders, backs, heads. A procession of townspeople interrupted the dim light of the shoes in pyramid, of hair and clothes in bales, the glitter of granary heaps of eyeglasses, watches, jewelry. Beneath the cold gaze of GIs, a few of the women were in tears, but most of the town faces were composed to show nothing, a blankness.

She caught sight of me and leapt up.

"Jasie, Jasie, what are you doing out here?"

I stammered. "I…I…"

The scrape of her chair on the floor startled me, and her movements were sudden and brisk. Hands fluttering, she switched off the set, the screen blackening to a star, a dot, and then nothing. She wiped her eyes with her palms and took me by the hand.

"Did you have a bad dream? Do you want a glass of water?"

Her cheeks were glazed with drying tears. Had my father heard? His sleep was delicate, forbidden to disturb. Was he even home yet? It couldn't have been so late. Of course he wasn't there. If he were, he'd have been lying beside her, the Castro Convertible sofa unfolded, the television off, the room even darker. My mother would have swung herself out of bed to bring me back as fast as she could, to quiet me, to give me the water I would ask for.

Once, some years later, when I came out of my bedroom he was there—naked from the waist down on his way to the toilet. I'd had other glimpses, fuller by then, of pictures, photographs, and films of the time of killing, which hadn't yet been given the name Holocaust. I had been astonished at that nakedness, which had become the property of the world, the limp ivory of limbs, my eyes drawn to the dark midpoint of the bodies, the undiminished pubis in the fork of the withered legs as they tumbled, bulldozed into the mass graves. The dark hair of his body was like what I had seen—their intimate hair like his. How was he here and not among them? His unfocus and dishevelment looked like anger to me even before I was sure it was. Had I wakened him so often when I was a child?

*My parents at Lincoln Terrace Park in Brooklyn, where they met for the first time in a chance encounter on the tennis courts*

My mother was the keeper of his sleep, and his companion griever. More than that, she made space for the grief, was always available for it, whether he was or not—and for the stories. She cleared the way for his, in part by telling none of her own and preserving so little from her immigrant parents, who had stories of the Pale that my father might have recognized as continuous with his. She filled in for the indifference of the world—the blank faces of the near-witnesses, those close by who refused to witness, forced to parade past the evidence. She was ever the helpless witness, guilty of not knowing what was happening to the Jews, a bystander in America. And her expiation was in vigilance and tears.

Just as I had been unsettled by her private tears in the darkened apartment, I would be disturbed by her tears in public. When I was in the fourth grade, I took part in a school concert. As I mounted the stage, one of a long line of classmates, I saw her, and no one else, crying. Embarrassed, I struggled to sing along: *midenah, midenah, l'ami hanoded*—a country, a country for my wandering people. But I knew the tears weren't for me. They were for the other children, the ones in the films and photographs. The tears were her faithfulness to them, almost all of them nowhere now. Dark clothing, pale faces—the well-known monochrome world of the little girl behind the wire who rolls up a sleeve and shows the number on her arm.

Among those gone children, I would imagine another child, a particular child, a better child than me, a boy my mother could easily love, never the occasion of a father's anger, always biddable, who loved his piano lessons, who would wear the clothes she chose for him without demur, who never considered them as unmasculine. Not that I thought of them in those terms. But I did feel betrayed by what she sent me out wearing, onto the streets of the Bronx. When I was three or four it was a sailor suit, which embarrassed me in retrospect, looking at the black-and-white snapshots. By six or seven I rebelled at the Bermuda shorts, the English schoolboy haircut. I knew I would be ridiculed and, more than that, endangered. The tough kids, the Irish kids, didn't like us, taught me the names kike, sheeny, Jew boy. Didn't she know that? How could she have floated above all that, my beloved bystander? Of course, the present dangers for me were so much less than the past ones for my father.

My difficulties may have been painful, but never fatal, and always instructive.

I don't think Tommy Sullivan and I ever called for one another. I never saw him at my door, or heard him calling for me from the backyard—like Lee, who would shout up through the clotheslines, oddly and occasionally way too early on a Sunday morning, "Jason's mother, Jason's mother, can Jason come out and play?" Tommy and I always met outside—never pre-arranged, which was unusual. He lived in the building, several floors up. It would have been natural for him to collect me sometimes on his way to the street. I didn't think about it, naive even for a child. Firmly entrenched in my own group, I didn't think much about groups, what they meant, or else I was right at the start of a conscious understanding, which Tommy would advance. My mother would say things about the Irish around us, many of them Irish born—how lovely the women were, their manner and speech—but that the men seemed rough to her. I learned that she meant the drinking particularly, and what sometimes came out of it.

I'd encounter Tommy on the front steps and we'd amble around or sit on the stoops flanking the passageway leading to the backyard, basement carriage room, and garbage cans. We would talk, too young for stickball or pitching baseball cards or pennies. In fall we could be dueling with chest-nuts strung on a shoelace, each of us alternating a swinging strike until only one chestnut survived. To consider who played with whom hadn't occurred to me, except in regard to girls out jumping rope to various rhyming accompaniments. Boys could watch them, but gender segregation was pretty much absolute. I knew so little about the girls' society I can't say whether the tribes mixed there.

Tommy and I talked on and off from when we were very young, starting with basic stuff like how long it took to count to a thousand. We would hear things about the Yankees. Mickey Mantle was vaguely a presence, though we didn't follow league standings. The stadium was close by but felt very distant, each neighborhood its own country. We had a very narrow sense of territory; several thousand people must have lived in the apart-ment houses on the street, but around the corner was terra incognita.

Tommy and I talked religion, as we progressed in the acculturation for which each was destined. I attended Akiba Academy and he was at Holy Spirit. I had God, one and indivisible, and lots of rules about what I could or couldn't eat. Tommy had three persons—father, son, and Holy Ghost—but one God, and how that was possible was a mystery. Not only couldn't

*Family portrait, circa 1953*

he explain it; it couldn't be explained. In one of these conversations, Tommy confided his discovery that one of the persons—the son, Jesus—was Jewish. He'd always assumed, as I had, that Jesus was Catholic. No great leap was involved in my next piece of reasoning. If Jesus had begun Jewish, and transferred, one way or another, to Catholicism, then the Sullivans, too, must have been Jewish at one time. I'm not sure whether I visualized an evolution over generations or conceived of individual metamorphoses in each generation. However it was, Tommy seemed persuaded. It made sense to him. We moved on to other topics.

Several days after that conversation, he suggested we play with some boys he knew around the block. I followed him into the courtyard of the first apartment house around the corner, where he greeted some kids who were standing around. One of them, a year or two older than us, was throwing a ball against the bricks below the windows. Suddenly Tommy turned and punched me in the stomach, very hard. I was doubled over, gagging; it hurt so much, so bowels-deep inside my body, and the pain came with such shock that I registered no betrayal. I had no sense of it then, any more than I could be sure my tears were not merely from retching. I was alone among strangers, who just stared. One boy came over and stood beside me. He didn't say anything, though I felt him as a sympathetic presence. Ashamed, exposed, I headed home as soon as I could straighten up and catch my breath, walking as fast as I could.

I avoided Tommy from then on, checking carefully through the doors before I went out. He must have kept away from me too. It seems obvious to me now that he had discussed our findings on the Jewish question with his family. Though I hadn't considered Tommy one of them, I had begun to understand about the Irish kids and learned to steer clear of the teenagers who hung around in a courtyard across the street, led by a bully named John. I wasn't yet sure what they had against me and some other neighborhood kids, but they often glowered and called out when I passed. I had told my mother what happened with Tommy, but we both knew not to say anything to my father. She would have had more reasons than I for caution, but vividly in my mind was an incident from the previous winter.

In the aftermath of a snowstorm, the street covered and traffic stilled, I'd been in and out of the apartment, changing wet clothes, breaking for lunch, and coming back down to play. However, my movements had been noted. As I stepped out of the doors, a barrage of snowballs hit my face, head, and chest. They were hardpacked with slush and I nearly fell, stunned long enough to be caught in another volley. Before I spun around to retreat inside, I saw the especially florid face of John, standing out among the three on the other side of the street. I ran up to the apartment in tears. When my father saw my face and heard about the ambush, he turned me around and brought me downstairs, the muscles in his jaw working. As we reached the entry, we could see through the glass of the doors, somewhat distorted by the thick panes, the trio across the street, standing behind a car that sat between snowdrifts. My father crossed to them at a run, leaving me behind propping one of the solid French doors with my shoulder. He barreled into them, and in moments two were on the ground, a hat near one and chunks of snow in his hair, the other with a face full of it. John was upended in the drift by the car's front bumper, a boot dangling from his foot.

My father's response bought me peace for quite a while. I couldn't help being pleased at his ferocity on my behalf, admiring the sheer force of him directed outward, but it also felt dangerous, unhinged. Other things happened, in other neighborhoods, somewhat sharper in focus, often with a theological question before encounters: Do you believe in…? Once, I swear, some jerk approached me and a friend with a catechetical question about the Assumption of the Blessed Virgin. Then, there had been the yarmulke calisthenics that took place around Akiba, my yeshiva: wearing our skullcaps we would be accosted by groups of boys who wanted to see how many times we would stoop, kiss them, and put them back on our heads when they fell—or rather were knocked off. We learned to remove the head coverings outside of school. These Irishers were my version of the stone-throwing peasant boys of my father's childhood, but his had grown up to gather into armies and carry guns. I can't say exactly when I had that thought, or when I knew that my being bullied was so much less, such a miniature that it shouldn't be mentioned in the same breath.

The dangers my dad had escaped seemed to have made him even more precious to my mother: the heaped bodies, all the dead in the films he had managed not to be among. For me, his survival was a thing to wonder at, to worry at. As I got older, that glimpse of film in the dark living room expanded to curated showings, a teacher's careful introduction, and then nightmare variations of the images. They had been increasingly available to me, to my mother, to anyone, from the late 1950s through the early '60s. Fragments of newsreels that had been in theaters were now on television: footage from the Eichmann trial, documentaries with their solemn voice-over and somber music. By then I had my library card and was a serious and precocious reader. At the library I could dig, unsupervised, unearthing what at home was forbidden. As time passed, in the natural course of things, adults said more in my hearing. My father was something of a raconteur and always found people willing to listen. Uncle Harry, too, my father's older brother, spoke sometimes of what had happened to him in the war, though his wife, my aunt Lilly, continued to refuse.

But the films, the early glimpses, were the touchstone for everything. The black-and-white, jumpy framing and uncertain lighting, the flawed surface of the film itself, added credibility, established those moving pictures as the truest record of the actual. They seemed so absolute somehow, so embedded in my mind. Everything that happened to my family, my father, would have to fit into them or seem counterfeit in some way. They served as the evidence for a child's logic, a syllogism that proceeded from a strange premise: The European Jews were dead Jews; my father was a European Jew, therefore...

The history I learned ought to have changed the way I saw the pictures, should have helped me understand that there were as many stories as there were faces in the photographs, and many other settings than the camps, other graves than the mass pits. But I resented my father and his special suffering, which crowded me out. His story alone became the story of the family. I was an item in compensation, a replacement for those he had lost; the *here and now* was always usurped by the *there and then*. But the films were so *substantive*, bearing the impossible weight of all those bodies. His survival seemed some kind of deception, oddly equivalent in my mind to my sense of the charm he directed at others.

My dad had many subplots to his story; he wasn't just a survivor and a storyteller constantly alert to the possibility of an audience. He spoke six languages by then—eventually it would be ten. He was an accomplished athlete and dancer. Almost in one breath, he learned English and enrolled in Brooklyn College—this was a man who hadn't even finished elementary school—and he completed his college education with classes in the evening and factory work in the day. He studied languages and secondary education and soon was recognized as a master teacher, eventually becoming New York State Teacher of the Year and then National Teacher of the Year. As I reached my teens, I was aware of the adoring teenagers who saw him differently from the way I did. He had a knack with adolescents (except for the one he lived with). He could radiate interest, asking about what someone studied, favorite subjects—the standard questions—but really seeming to listen, and then he would always do some proselytizing for foreign language study. He'd tell an escape story, how languages saved his life.

At fifteen, I was ripe with this resentment. Part of it was simple adolescent rebelliousness, but nothing was simple in the shadow of my father's narrative.

It came to a head one Saturday in October. I had engineered, without much forethought, an end to the additional Hebrew school classes I was taking at Schiff Center. I simply stopped going. I would leave the house as for the classes and ride my bike until it was a plausible time to return. I hadn't attended for weeks. No one was the wiser. Until that Saturday.

Arriving home to our Kingsbridge apartment, I found him standing in the middle of the kitchen with a letter in his hand. He was fuming. He waved the paper at me, his jaw clenching and unclenching.

"What's this?"

The heading on the paper was visible, even in motion, and though I had pushed awareness away, I saw then that I had expected this reckoning. I said nothing.

"What's this?" he repeated.

"Why the hell don't you tell me?" I said. "You're the one reading it."

And that was it. He was fully ignited.

"Goddamn it, *yah*," he said as he lunged for me. I dodged his grasp and we were off to what must have looked like a slapstick chase. Our narrow kitchen opened two ways into the living room, and if I kept running around the circuit I could keep ahead of him. For a time, anyway, a couple of loops—he was still faster than I was and stronger. Except I didn't keep running. I stopped, turned, and put up my fists. He too stopped and stared at me. We both knew what we were on the brink of—and that there would be no way back from it. He looked hard at me for a moment, saying nothing. Then he went back to his bedroom, and I left the house for a while. He never tried to hit me again.

His anger didn't disappear. I would still shiver at the volume of his voice rising to it. But that was the end of physical discipline. Though not the end of my resentment.

Soon afterward I read or heard something that gave shape to my own anger. So many had been killed in the Holocaust, how could he not be among them? What had he done to escape that inevitable fate? So recently in flight from his anger, I constructed a cruel fantasy that, in a strange way, seemed to free me from his influence. And that false freedom prompted me to share this callow daydream outside the family.

My junior-high friend Bobby was Jewish like me but from the heights, Riverdale, uphill and up-income from where I lived. Bobby had had his bar mitzvah ceremony at a Reform temple, with a lavish reception somewhere else. I was jealous, not of his party at that banquet hall (I was enough my mother's son to consider it vulgar) but of how he had been allowed to treat the whole business not so much as initiation but rather as exit exam. Mine had been modest, at a much stricter synagogue with a small reception on site and my Jewish education unrelieved. Even after I left yeshiva for public school, I'd had to enroll in hated after-school school, and then Jewish high school. But that was now over. I was free of it, had freed myself, hadn't allowed my father to compel me.

Bobby and I were in his huge room, with its view of the Hudson, sitting on his bed, taking turns trying to form bar chords on his guitar. He was talking about his future. And his father, who was a doctor, as his grandfather had been. So would Bobby become one?

"Yeah, it could be interesting. Though he's out a lot, you know, working all the time. And it's kind of a lot of school, more school, to get to be one."

He strained at a B-flat, dropping his shoulder and curving his wrist under the neck of the guitar.

I said, "I think—I sometimes think—my father was a Nazi."

The guitar went silent. Bobby dropped his hand from the neck and turned from the waist to face me. He knew my dad. Liked him, as most kids my age did.

"Jesus, what the fuck are you talking about?"

"That he's no survivor, not even a Jew. His bad sleeping is conscience and he's in disguise, sort of."

Bobby kept looking at me like I was crazy, which in a way I was.

"What happened—did you…? Are you on drugs?"

"No, listen, I read about these guards…. When the Americans were coming, or the Russians, and the camps were just coming apart, they escaped by disguising themselves as Jews, putting on the striped pajamas or disguising themselves other ways. Not only that. They lived as Jews afterwards. A way they did atonement, maybe. But sometimes the way they were, well, it showed through."

"Oh, come on. But congratulations, Sommer, that is some of the craziest bullshit I have ever heard. Your father is no Nazi on the run."

Even as I said it, though, even as I told the evil theory, the fantasy, I was aware of how much I had transgressed. Even then I wondered what could right that kind of wrong, thinking such a thing, saying it. To an outsider. A reason to try and imagine my father's actual life. Another reason to accept and share in what Jewishness I could manage.

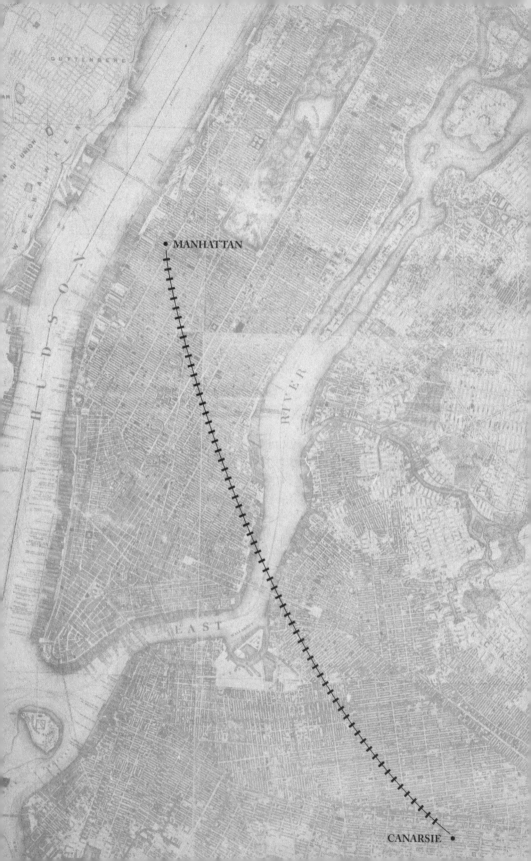

# 3

*refreshed in the knowledge*

*that what has been given me is given*
*in the grant of other people's survival,*
*hard won and conferring on them*

*the power of occasional contempt,*

. . . . . . . . . . . . . . . . . . . . .

*sufficiently blessed*
*that the places of my exile are so close to home*

THE FIRST TIME I NOTICED was in an aside, in something my Uncle Harry said to my father in an exchange in Hungarian. I heard a word stand out, as one of the few things I could understand: a name, Shmiel, Samuel. And there was a little shock of recognition. That was what they called him. The third brother. The youngest. The one I never knew. The one who didn't survive.

I had been saying his name wrong. I had taken to calling him Shmuel— had done so for a long time. And he answered to the name, not personally of course, but through my father and Harry when I spoke about him, especially in the lead-up to our 2001 trip. The linguistic fluidities of their home region aside, this acceptance represented something else. They had never corrected me, never said a word. Sometimes they called him that too, when we talked about him together. But Shmuel is the Hebrew version of the name and unlikely, when they were young, to have been used anywhere but the synagogue. Only in that place would he have been Shmuel Ben Eliahu, as my father was Melech Ben Eliahu in shul and Meilech in daily life.

Shmiel was Yiddish, the version in the *mamaloshen*, the mother tongue, a single syllable in the speech of his own mother, Yitta Feiga.

I hadn't made the change deliberately, but I was aware how transformations were marked. My Hebrew-schooled head was full of the lore. Jacob became Israel, after he contended with the angel—the "el" suffix refers to the most ancient name of God. The new name came with the charge of living out a new and changed life. Yet I wouldn't have featured myself as the bestower of new names, nor did I think what had happened to him had anything to do with God, or martyrdom either.

The more I had learned of him, the more he stood apart in my mind. Some of that was the gradual, tantalizing way that details emerged. Information came little by little over years, haphazardly, but was in general dictated by a combined consideration for the age of the children present and the survivor's tolerance for remembering at a given moment. I had learned not to press. My father and my uncle spoke of him lovingly, but with few specifics. So each detail—each of the few details—were precious and surrounded with the effort to imagine more, to make a fuller picture of the boy who, though the youngest brother, grew into the tallest and strongest, who protected my father from physical violence with physical violence of his own.

When gentile friends asked me about Jewish resistance (and only the closest would ask), I had pat answers. My dear Irish friends especially, during my years living in Dublin, would ask directly, artlessly, why Jews had allowed themselves to be carried off to their deaths. I would answer that there *had* been resistance, which came in various forms: revolts, subversion, partisan defiance. But I knew what they were asking. In the ghettos, at the roundups—with children present—even a futile resistance would require conviction about what was in store. I would say all that; I would say that it took calories to resist.

I said these things, but I admired Shmuel because he had refused to acquiesce, he made the attempt, he contended. For me the Hebrew version of my uncle's name was redolent not of the synagogue or Bible story but of Israel, the state. With the foundation of a Jewish state came at least the perception of a revival of elements in the Jewish character that had been largely absent for several thousand years. Yiddish names were for the hounded. I am aware this makes much of my uncle's doomed effort, but the state of Israel at its very inception provided Jews, Jewish men in particular, with a model for a restored masculinity. Leaving aside current politics and policies, for Jewish children raised in the fifties and sixties, a different model of Jew emerged with Israel, born in part out of the study of war. For me, one of the least tough kids in the Bronx, masculinity could be defined simply as the ability to respond to bullying with effective violence. This was not quite what my uncle had done, but I believed he would have, that what he did do was somewhere on a continuum toward that idea. I believed, too, that my father and my uncle Harry must have understood how Shmuel was right for Samuel.

What my uncle had done. What had happened on the rail bridge on the line to Auschwitz. Precisely where that bridge was and what I could do to get to it with my father, to stand on its deck, if possible, and, sixty years after the fact, enable my father to…to what? Grieve? Curse? Commemorate?

These were the fragments that ran through my mind in the months leading up to our 2001 trip. Along with other shards of family experience, having to do with names and their mutability, that had occupied me for decades.

My aunt Lilly never spoke of Auschwitz and wouldn't have it spoken of around her. At least not in the late 1960s, when I would occasionally visit her and my uncle Harry at their home. They were Lilly and Harry Muller, Harry having taken my grandmother's maiden name after his own father died and his stepfather deserted. Surnames also had some fluidity too, though I hadn't considered the matter very much then. The visits I saw as duty calls at the time, a college kid with more important things to do. I had to present myself in Brooklyn or give offense. Harry was my dad's beloved surviving brother, and the insult would have been to my father too. Besides, I did have my own feeling for them.

Canarsie, though, was the literal end of the line, and felt like the end of the earth to me, as its name once signified: *by way of Canarsie*. I'd heard tales of the mob dumping bodies in its marshes, but the only evidence of criminality was the train, which had been elaborately and unreadably graffitied in the style of the time. This occasion was a solo visit, my parents

*Aunt Lilly with her daughter Bertha, one of a set family portraits taken soon after their arrival in America*

away, Lilly and Harry aware that I was in the city for the summer. I looked through sweeps of paint darkening the train window, making twilight of the late afternoon sun. Pulling into the station, I thought I could glimpse heaved asphalt, the street undulating with the bogginess of the reclaimed ground beneath.

My sense that I had bestowed myself, deigning to travel here, no doubt contributed to my attitude during dinner, as did the largely unspoken view of their house that my mother had communicated. My American-born mother cultivated taste, a modern taste as distant as she could manage from that of her own immigrant parents, who also were survivors though of earlier calamities. The brick duplex on Avenue J stood in a row of identical attached houses—one flight up to a door on a cement porch shaded by a metal awning. But it wasn't the architecture so much as the décor that I understood as not up to her standard. My family, the three of us, Bronx apartment-dwellers, hadn't lived in a house of our own, but my mother made it clear that when we did, it wouldn't be this sort. By following her eyes as we stepped through the door behind my father, I was alerted to the clichés of greenhorn decorating. Subtly, her gaze would flit across the offending details: the brocaded fabric of the sofa, under plastic sheathing; the photographs of my three cousins printed on canvas; the thick, tasseled drapes; the coffee table like a marble plinth, offering its bowl of wax fruit.

That evening, I probably saw the dinner as clichéd too, ethnic standard from chicken-soup start to honey-cake finish, though my aunt was an excellent cook, her *knaidlach* perfect, brisket that cut with a fork. It was the Ashkenazi food of my grandparents, and I took an unconsidered pleasure in it, especially after months of college cafeteria meals and my own miserable efforts in a roach-prone sublet. The Shabbos prayer that began the meal brought me among and not above them for a while.

My aunt, who could be fierce in silence, or silencing, also seemed calmed or somehow in abeyance that evening, the briskness of her motion to and from the kitchen stilled for the moments of the lighting of the candles. Once the two wicks caught, she dropped the match in a tray, lifted her hands, and brought them toward her face three times, her fingers spread like the wing tips on a large bird, steadying for a landing. She covered her eyes as she said the prayer. My uncle made kiddish, blessing the wine and the braided challah, whose eggy glaze reflected the candlelight.

Conversation over the meal was typically sporadic, mostly in praise of the food. Some inquiry about what my parents were up to. Most of the talk was later on, around the table. They asked about my studies, my life. Harry was usually genial and mild, given to corny jokes, but that night I indulged in the secular ramblings that so annoyed him. I took the opportunity to raise consciousness, talking about freedom, on the continuum from personal emancipation at home right through to my admittedly small contribution to freedom in Vietnam—freedom from the lies of murderous governments, ours and theirs, and the war. My classes. My East Village summer sublet with a girlfriend, a dancer. And I was full of information on my activities at college, demonstrations against the war especially, and how I was going to continue what I'd begun in Boston for these New York months. Aside from the work, the couple of jobs I had lined up, I had some serious plans, travel too, though I needed to put together some money first.

"Jason Sommer, Jason Sommer, Jason Sommer's summer plans." My uncle broke in, singsonging.

I'd heard the tone before, though there was a new sharpness. Communicating almost by itself, never mind the words. The tone told me what a luxury item I was. No one could afford me, least of all me, myself—an American, an American child, an ignorance, a softness.

"Jason Sommer, you think *that* is your name?" he went on. Lilly's face grew stony, serious about the secrets of others as well as her own. As my uncle began his corrective, she hissed with her own sharpness, in that particular way she had, using his old-country name: *Herschel, du herst*—"Do you hear me, are you listening?"

But he continued. "Maybe the man who had it didn't need it anymore, and so your father took it."

She leveled another burst of Yiddish and the subject lapsed along with any chance for the evening to recover. Almost before he finished speaking, my mind had focused on a trip to Canada we'd taken, my father, my mother, and me, when I was a child. My dad's voice in reply to the border guard's question: Where had he been born? Breslau, Germany, he said. Even as a young boy, I knew well he had been born in Kustanovice. He was lying. Now I knew why. Though not the details. And I couldn't ask my uncle. I knew that what he'd said was true, but I also knew the etiquette around survivors. They could speak or not, as they wished, but it was forbidden to ask for more than what they'd told, if they had finished speaking.

I couldn't exactly say what came afterward: what stays with me all these years later is how the rhythm of the train back to Manhattan—*ticcuh ticcuh, ticcuh ticcuh*—began or intensified some sort of state I had entered. My name wasn't my name. Had I suspected it? Had I wanted the sort of name it had become? Not so overtly Jewish. I wandered the streets downtown with my perception skewed. A fog of things passed, alternately blurred or too sharp when in focus: poles and posts outlined in a sizzling aura, and the things themselves rendered two-dimensional. The words on signs on streets and stores I saw with wonderful clarity but couldn't really read or make sense of. More fog and more objects slicing through it, not lifting it but opening a clearing, a little space around whatever it was.

I wonder now, fifty years on, is this anything like my father's fog—the fog that has descended on him before he rises into it? At ninety-eight he can form no new memories and is also losing the past, which he preserved with such energy, which he strove to recover in mind and be compensated for in the world. The old sharpnesses of his life have begun to lose their edge in what I imagine as fog. Is that why he urged me to take this trip? Did he know it was coming? Or was the impetus for our journey always there, waiting for a softening in my resistance, a trust in him that I would honor what he wanted me to?

Names and their mysteries continued to fascinate and frighten: Sommer, Shmuel; Kustanovice, Munkacs. From college boy to grown man and into fatherhood, I negotiated these mysteries at arm's length, as it were, reluctant to press for testimony from those who would suffer to share it, but more desperate as time passed for the critical details that might help me assemble the truths I needed to understand my own history.

We were sitting around a table fully leafed out to accommodate Thanksgiving dinner at my parents' house. It was sometime in the early 1990s, twenty-five years after that other dinner, when Harry let slip the truth about my name. There was as much silver and glassware as I had ever seen there, including a spread of forks I was not sure how to apply. My mother had pulled out all the stops. The fare was American traditional with a nod toward Eastern Europe in the side dishes. Belts had been loosened and the talk was casual. And in English, mostly, though with Harry and Lilly present, bursts of Hungarian were liable to occur, along with the inevitable strands of Yiddish.

"Harry, I think it's fine as it is."

In spite of this protest from my mother, my uncle was up from the table and out to the foyer closet, to his overcoat, presumably. Quickly back, he stood across from her with a cloth tape measure and something white in the same hand, and waved toward her with the other, as if splashing water.

"You think, you think, Shirley. Just get the coat. Pat Nixon's people listened easier than you."

He didn't mention it much, but he'd made the red coat the former First Lady wore on the famous China trip and, with good humor, brought out this detail as reinforcement in the face of my mother's reluctance to fetch the coat he'd made for her. When she'd modeled it earlier, he had seen something that needed adjustment.

"Really, Harry..."

"*Chochema, yah; schneider, nisht,*" he said, and even Lilly laughed at the Yiddish. "A smart person, yes; a tailor, no."

And my mother sighed, joined in the laughter, and rose from the table to get the coat.

Harry had been doing well at his work, expressing particular satisfaction with the fall season and his conversion of the latest haute couture into a line of ready-to-wear. He was a master tailor, and once upon a time, a forced-labor time, a great deal depended on his skill with the uniforms of his overseers. Such a gathering as this was rarer than it had been. My cousin Steven lived abroad, and his older sister, Bertha, was in Oregon in a commune, though her two children were in New York with their father. Jay, the youngest of my three cousins, was there, though, and had been speaking about his research, something to do with the retina.

It was a time when stories were told, there at the table, though only if the tellers were so moved. But I was determined to move them, to break the etiquette by asking something. That's what had me nervous, if intent. The rules had never really been articulated, except on occasions when Lilly called a halt to certain conversations. It was nevertheless clear to me that no one should ask directly of survivors anything that might cause them pain to recall.

In my forties then, I still struggled to feel like an adult among them. I reminded myself that I had children of my own; too antsy to remain at the table, they had retreated to the basement, and their mother and my mother had gone off to look in on them. But I'd stayed behind with some purpose, feeling a bit childish, not so much to be asking a question but to be demanding a story, the full version, whatever details they had. But it was precisely my adulthood, my insistence on it, that allowed me. I felt obscurely that I had a right, that I had paid a certain price. Besides, I had some skills and had begun to learn some things already that might be of interest to them, might help them. I had something to give in exchange for my demand.

I said, "I wanted to ask about Shmuel." But I didn't know exactly what, at that moment, I did wish to ask, or rather how to make a start. Over the years I had heard of him, my dad's brother, half-brother to Harry, adored by both. My first clear recollection of hearing about another brother was as a child, eight or nine years old. When my father lit the yahrzeit candle for his mother—on the anniversary of her death, reckoned by the Hebrew calendar—he mentioned, sadly, to my mother that he didn't know his brother's yahrzeit.

It seemed a technicality; the death day was unknown so the candle was unlit. There should have been a way to give them that date. By the year of that Thanksgiving meal I had begun some research and wanted whatever facts they could provide to go with bits and pieces that felt like a tale. The kid brother of their childhoods, my father and Harry. I had only to mention the name, avoiding Lilly's eyes as I did. I knew this mention would bring us to the war, and there was a momentary pause, perhaps in deference to Lilly, whom everyone acknowledged had faced the worst of all of them. Her experience drew a line that was hard to cross. But they didn't cross it, beginning instead with versions of what I'd heard before.

My father spoke first: "He was so tall like you, and always in the woods."

"Then not like me," I said.

"You liked the country, Schroon Lake and camp."

"Yes, but not the woods. I found them a little scary, those hikes, the animal noises…"

"Always with animals, Shmuel, bringing home birds, rabbits, when he was six years, eight years."

"To eat? You were so poor." I was well aware this wasn't what he meant, but I wanted to change the course of conversation.

He shot me a look. "No, for pets, to heal them. Sometimes they just came to him, like he could speak to them."

"And the cat Miriam," Harry said, "he made her do things no one else could. She would play with a stick like a dog, bringing it back to him."

"Ah, Shmielcoo, he was strong, even as a child. Brave, too, going to get wood."

*Dad, center, still wearing the remnants of his uniform, and his brother Harry with snowball, in the Cremona camp*

"He'd drag back logs as big as he was," Harry said.

"And not afraid to go where he wasn't supposed to, if he could get wood. They had there, how do you call them, guards on the land. And if they caught you, you'd get a beating for sure and then maybe taken to the gendarmes."

"So, it made sense that he tried to escape the Germans," I said. "As he did."

I waited for Lilly to object, sure that she would. She had brothers of her own who were lost, along with her parents and other family, at their arrival at the railhead in Auschwitz-Birkenau. She had been engaged to Harry before he was taken away for forced labor and knew Shmuel from Munkacs.

From my dad's passing references to him, I'd always imagined Shmuel as half-wild himself, a forest creature who would have gnawed a limb off rather than stay in the trap. But it was a life he gnawed away, working at the wire meshed over the window of, not a cattle car—as one often heard—but a Karlsruhe freight train, a hundred tons, numbers chalked on the outside, on its way to Auschwitz. He forced himself out and dropped down—how far?—into water. Which water? The missing particulars had come to mean so much for me. I'd thought of him as a hero and I thought I could rescue his memory somehow, tether it—him—with facts from the drift of memory, save him even from the early myth.

Lilly said nothing.

My mother had returned from the basement, just in time to hear what I'd begun, and stood by the doorway, staring at me.

Nervous, I dove into the silence, chattering, filling the air with talk as I moved some plates to the sideboard to free some space for the atlas I said I was going to get. I had been looking at it in the sunroom. Just a second. I would run. There and back. Less than a minute. I did. No one moved.

On a clearing near the head of the table, at the corner between my father and uncle, I laid the oversized book, open at a map of Eastern Europe. It nearly slipped off the edge, and I steadied it, shoving it along the table so that the tablecloth bunched beneath it, tipping a glass, which my father caught. He rose and stood beside me, looking down at the map.

"So, you can see," I said, "it's a little hard, but those are the rail lines in black with the small crossed lines like dashes across them. And here—I know it's faint—the blue lines are the rivers. The red lettering is the names: the Latorica, which runs through the city."

"Latorica." My father echoed the name faintly. I thought of how he studied, sometimes reading aloud.

"The Tisza. That would be too soon out of Munkacs."

"Tisza," my dad said, continuing the soft echo.

"Laborec."

"Laborech." I had used a hard "c" and my father's repetition corrected it to "ch."

"Ondava."

"Ondava."

"Topl'a."

"Topl'a."

"Torysa."

"Torysa."

The names were like an incantation. As if we were chanting, a slightly overlapping call and response, trying to say, together almost, the name of each river to flow against the current of forgetting.

"But I don't know yet. Anyway, I had this idea, if I just follow the rivers until the lines of the tracks cross them—or maybe it should be the other way around—I'll have the place. I have better maps of the train routes, and there's something called the Auschwitz Kalendarium. SS diaries too. I'm not sure how fast the trains went, but—you know—rate by time equals distance, and I think I could get the date the transport left and do some figuring that way."

Truly, I was babbling, wanting someone to respond in some way, if only to halt my own onrush. But I careered on.

"With all the transfer of the land, I got the nationality wrong at first for Munkacs—when I was looking for the time of the deportations. And I had it in mind anyway that it was winter, stuck on some movie scene: a shot man rolling down an incline into snow. I don't know how that got—"

"May," Lilly said, abruptly.

I went silent.

"May," she repeated, "between the twentieth and the twenty-second. Two days, two nights from the brickworks. We went the same train."

She had been on that transport. She had been there. I looked around and nobody appeared stunned that she had harbored this fact for more nearly fifty years. Was nobody going to ask anything? I kept at her, resolute to retrieve what I could of the hero from the silence, her long silence. How could she not have said?

"Lilly, which was it then? I mean, there was shooting. The train was stopped on a railway bridge, right? So was it the twentieth or the twenty-first. Day? Night?"

How could she not know? The shrieking of the brakes, *polizei* shouting in German, the splashing in the water. She must have remembered the day.

She was almost gentle in her response: "No, there was shooting many times; many times the train would stop without a reason a long time. In our car, everyone, old people and children, were pressed together. We women held rags out of the window to catch rainwater to drink. The train had many cars. No one thing happened I could tell from where I was."

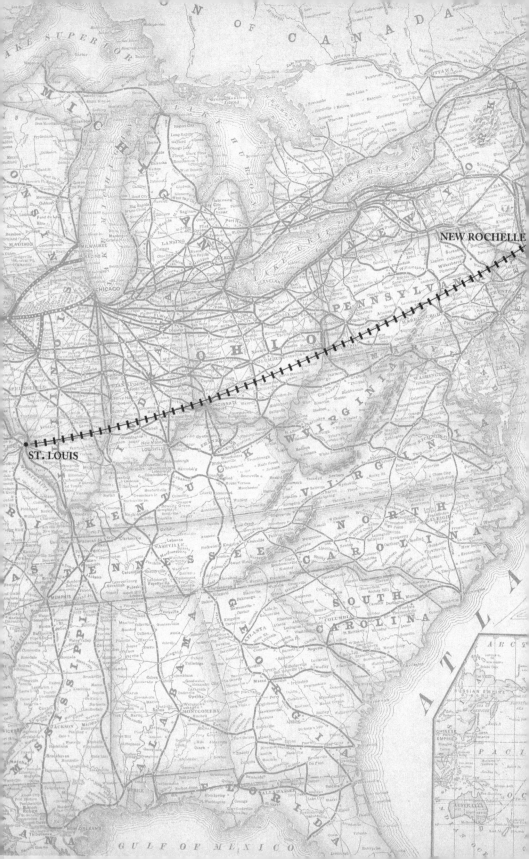

# 4

*I want whatever else can be recovered*
*to hold Shmuel at the center of a final scene*

. . . . . . . . . . . . . . . . . . . . . . . . . .

*I want the discipline of facts,*
*about that train to Auschwitz, to anchor Shmuel*
*in the drift of others' memory where he swims*
*across an unnamed river to his death*
*in a flood of gunfire on the farther shore.*

TEN YEARS WOULD PASS between Aunt Lilly's Thanksgiving revelation and my trip to Eastern Europe with my father. The lines above are from a long poem I published at the midpoint of that decade, as I worked imaginatively to confront the history of my family's passage through the European fire and to define my own quest for the right way to question and puzzle and interpret. To find a way to join the stories of survivors and a survivor's son.

But it took that full span of time to get to where I was braced to visit, with my dad, the settings of the stories he had told so often over the years: the place where he was born and raised; the various places where, by all odds, he should have been killed, but which he managed either to avoid or to pass through physically unharmed; and, if we could find it, the place where Shmuel was killed.

Yet even then, in the spring of 2001, I wasn't entirely certain I was ready.

I was concluding a busy semester in anticipation of a coming sabbatical, a full year to be devoted to writing. It had been several years since my last book, and so much work was unfinished, deferred to the urgencies of teaching, earning a living, caring for children. But I was also conscious of other long deferrals, other urgencies. Though eager to start the year of writing, I considered beginning the sabbatical with the trip with my father.

As we discussed the prospect that spring, I began to feel a general willingness to go and, more than that, the approach of a kind of natural moment, a sense that my own life had gathered enough substance of its own to allow further immersion in his without dissolving. Or maybe I was simply willing to disappear for a while, sufficiently secure in my early fifties that I could reappear later. My father had always wanted me to show the sort of interest in his life story that a visit to its settings would evidence. And I was apparently ready to do that, after long avoidance, even resistance. But I was proposing something in addition: not so much an added dimension as a kind of reversal of field, as I see now. We would be visiting my father's places because they were not his alone, and a central purpose of our travels would concern Shmuel. And for me necessarily, because of my ongoing research, my energies before we left would have to focus on what happened to the dead brother and where. A number of questions needed answers if I, if we, were to succeed.

I have never been certain whether my father ever read the poem, quoted above, in which I speak about what would constitute success in its most obvious form—that is, discovering the place where Shmuel attempted his escape from the train to Auschwitz. In the poem itself the bet is hedged. The lines that promise to find the bridge are qualified: "I have a plan to follow rivers/ if only on the maps." In these verses I did not commit myself, and certainly not my father, to planes and trains and automobiles. The poem made my interest clear, the fact of it, and even some of its elements: my longing, for a start, to have the lost person emerge from a kind of myth, and from the fog of memory.

My dad wasn't much for poetry, though every now and then I would hear from friends of his that he had shown them an early one of mine, "The Ballad of Fighting with My Father," which centered around a pair of brass swords he'd made for us from bits and pieces he'd brought home from his job in a lamp factory and which had lent a clanging reality to childhood duels. For him the poem was a simple tribute; for me an exploration of Oedipal conflict, with a real, if only semiconscious, attempt by the child, by me, to inflict harm toward the end of the encounter.

38

But whatever about the poems, I wanted this trip to be a chance for us to share a conscious understanding, an agreement on a plot I would propose, translated to itinerary, that both of us could be comfortable with. Whatever Shmuel had come to mean for me, he was my father's brother, whose loss was among his deepest griefs.

In our discussions of the trip, I sensed a stew of motives in myself, though I wouldn't have been able to identify the ingredients definitively. Initially I had said yes to his idea of the journey and then reduced his idea to a component of another journey. That nagged at me a little. Just a little. Still, I felt I needed to be convinced that it was something he wanted and felt able to do, that the search for the location of Shmuel's final moments was his project now as much as mine. He was vigorous at seventy-eight, often taken for much younger, but it wasn't his physical condition that concerned me. I suppose I was looking to evade feelings of responsibility for what did concern me, what pain my idea might cause.

As spring came closer to summer, I called him from my home in St. Louis.

"Are you sure about our flying off together," I asked, "doing what we're going to do? You know, Budapest, Munkacs—the thing with Shmuel."

Even over the phone I could sense his surprise.

"Jase, I have many things done already. The travel agent is only waiting for us for dates. Is there something...?"

"No. No, I was just wondering whether you had any second thoughts, whether it was too..."

"For what? We decide how many days—we can later today; what time is it now?—and then with the email write Eva in Budapest. She can get for us the train tickets. It's better to do from there. Incidentally, we have already someone to drive in Ukraine."

He was all-go. And that shouldn't have surprised me; my dad never wavered in such circumstances. He would speak about the practicalities, say what he had done but not how he felt about anything. So we decided: we would leave at the end of May. *My* approval was the last step. Inwardly I was relieved, half-afraid he would ask me why I was so set on the part about Shmuel, and how was that going to be possible for us to do, really? I had counted on the reason for our small quest being self-evident to him somehow, and I wouldn't have indulged in any complicated explanation, but the simplest response to the question of why do it, the most self-evident—to honor his brother's memory or whatever his articulation of that would have been—might have been for me almost like a lie.

The other part of the unasked question, the how, how would we find the place, was tacitly left to me, I understood.

I arrived in New York in mid-May, a week before our departure for Budapest. A heat wave made the season feel more like late summer than late spring, and, making my way to my parents' house in New Rochelle, I had a sort of momentary spasm of consciousness. I felt as if we had missed the interval planned for travel, that time had jump-cut past, right into the mugginess of the start of fall semester. He would be returning to the adjunct college teaching he'd made a second career. I would be back teaching, myself—my climate-induced pang apparently removed my sabbatical as well but passed quickly.

Our travel papers had been arranged by a visa service. We agreed it was worth the expense to make sure we could actually cross the borders we intended to and, additionally, not risk our passports in the mail or hauling ourselves to the embassies of four different countries in person. I had communicated a simple plan to my father, which he had passed along to his contacts in Hungary: from Budapest we would travel to Munkacs and from there follow the tracks to Auschwitz—the method I had articulated in my poem. A simple plan. Only thing was, for starters, which tracks? There were two routes. One of them dipped south and went through Slovakia; the other headed north, entered Poland near Uzhhorod going through Lviv. Which had Lilly and Shmuel's transport taken? How many bridges were there, and would we be able to get to them by road?

That week I buried myself in maps. But I had little to go on. Lilly had never indicated how they had traveled in that transport. She had no idea. Some time ago she had made an offhand reference to a Munkacs couple, also Auschwitz survivors, and my dad and I had trekked out to Brooklyn, where we were welcomed by a perfectly lovely pair with little in common with my father but the town. A few years younger than he, Hungarian speakers, they came from a prosperous family, streets and a world away from my father's grinding poverty. There was some talk of the national shifts, as there always was with the town—they too had been born Czech

*Dad and Mom dancing at a wedding in 1974. If they were attending a wedding, my parents would be dancing.*

and ended up Hungarian, never having left Mukachevo. The husband said that his last memory of anything Czech back then had been in a cattle car in Slovakia, where he heard the language spoken through the "cracks" on the side of the wagon and even glimpsed some town names.

I had found other survivor testimony, several other people from Munk-acs on the May transports, who made direct mention of Košice, Slovakia, as a place they recognized—and as the place where German guards took over from Hungarian gendarmes. I remember the shock of that, being reminded that it was principally Hungarians who rounded up and loaded the Jews on the freight cars. But it was also the beginning of a kind of relief about the railway line. Here was one definite lead. But it wasn't the certainty I craved. For now, though, the sensible thing to do would be to concentrate on the Slovakian route.

At my parents' house, maps lay unfolded on the desks and over the floor, in opened books, in bookmarked travel guides, even online. I'd hauled books and papers to New York from St. Louis and added others while in New York. The maps tantalized and frustrated as I pored over them, going from one to another, head spinning. I searched for towns to orient myself and then for rivers, railways. On most, the smaller town and river names were simply hard to make out, often in minuscule type. Especially difficult to locate were the junctions where rail lines intersected rivers, which I was most eager to locate. It appeared that often the tracks meandered with the river rather than crossing it. The straight lines were few and far between. I supposed that made sense, as a bridging would have been more difficult, and more expensive, than laying track.

In what promised to be a eureka moment, I discovered a wonderful map detailing the railway bridges of Slovakia, on an official Slovakian railway website. Unfortunately, only the rail lines and little rectangles that marked the bridges were represented. No towns, no rivers. Excited nevertheless, I ran to get my father. Together we went over it, cross-referencing it to maps with fuller topographical detail. This new map identified routes with two village names paired by dashes. The Košice–Presov line leapt out at me; Košice would come up again and again. There were also notes included about each rail line, everything in Czech, as well as dimensions of some sort and lots of bridges.

"Dad, what is this word: must be 'bridge,' right?"

"Yes, that's 'bridge.'"

"And this, this before the numbers here?"

"Ah, 'opening'—yes, 'opening.'"

"Opening, what opening? What sense does that make? And this here, the twenty-five meters must be the span. There is a single track here."

"Jase, I'm a language teacher, not an engineer—and there's the Czech dictionary over there."

"Wait, wait. It's dated 1945." I scrolled down the page, pointed to some words by the date. My father translated the Czech:

"'The partisans, they…exploded the bridge.'"

"Crap, exploded bridges."

I had never even considered that, sabotage. But I could see "Bratislava" in the next few lines. So that bridge was too far west anyway. But where else had there been partisans or Russians or perhaps Hungarians or Germans destroying the bridges for whatever military reasons, covering their retreat?

I kept at my calculations right up to the eve of our departure. I noted the vitals of the bridges, even when I wasn't quite sure what the measurements represented. I combined maps as best I could. I did some work with maps of Poland, including the eastern part, which I nevertheless prayed had been eliminated. The Slovakian route crossed into Poland too, of course. All the roads, rail or tar, led to Auschwitz in this journey.

*There's the Czech dictionary over there.* Dictionaries also filled the house in New Rochelle, reminding me of my dad's gift for languages and how I would be depending on him on this trip for translation—on top of the emotional freight of the visits themselves, of the search for the bridge, of the challenge I had posed myself to align, and compare, Dad's stories with the concrete details of their landscapes.

And then there were my own settings. Leaving St. Louis, I had told friends that I was going home, but I had never lived in suburban New Rochelle, the brick-and-stucco Tudor among other single-family homes with lawns and sidewalks buckling from the upthrust of tree roots. This was my parents' house, their escape from the Bronx, an arrival in the America they had imagined like so many others of their background. I had grown up in our Bronx apartments, where my dad and I had learned English together in the 1950s, where my mother brought me out of babble to words, while he, with her help, was adding English to his other languages.

At that time my mother was becoming a teacher, subbing at first though still at home most of the time, teaching both of us to speak properly. Teaching us the permanent and fixed values of the language of literature, the classics that will always be classics, the manners that are everlasting, the pronunciation that is standard. "Not *p'yance*, for heaven's sake, but *pants*, Jason." Over and over. Outside of the family, my father was often pleased to be noticed for his accent, an opening for contact with other people, and laughter was his least favorite form of correction, especially from us. Nevertheless, my mother and I would sometimes giggle at his vowel juggling—once, famously, at his diagnosis of our off-kilter car's broken "shack obsorbers."

*My father at ninety*

When visiting New Rochelle without my family, I camped in my dad's small study, surrounded by its tall bookshelves, full of those dictionaries and other books, many with titles in Cyrillic and Semitic script. One night during that week before departure, the unseasonable New York heat oppressive, I lay on the couch that was my bed, idly watching a film on the small black-and-white TV wedged onto one of the bookshelves, and nodding off and on. The windows were open, and the room felt continuous with night yet sealed, all contained in some giant humidor, dense with small sounds: the trilling of crickets or katydids, and some other unidentifiable creature making an odd call. It wasn't the first time I had tried to find a name for that thing and its sound, if only when I drowsed in this room on this couch.

Half-asleep seemed right for this house, for my return to the bare triangle of a family always liable to have dreams outside of the bed. We were night travelers in our own habitations. More and more, and long before her retirement, my mother wandered from the ordinary diurnal rhythms and could be washing dishes at two in the morning. My father often slept badly, his past most likely to disturb him then, dreams of being pursued that pursued him year after year, along with the losses. All through my early childhood he'd materialize by crib or cot at some late hour for us to have a glimpse of each other. Those appearances were not insomniac but the result of his being kept away by his education, most of which happened in the evening. Even when I was much older, in our second neighborhood farther north in the Bronx, I'd be in from college, returning home from a night downtown with friends, and I would see him in the short corridor on his way back to their bedroom, his pale face floating in the dimness, his look perhaps an accusation I could barely make out, disapproval at my staying out so late, or maybe merely the distracted expression of interrupted sleep.

I lay in the heat, half-listening to the night creature, balanced on what felt like both the brink of discovery and the edge of sleep, drifting over and then jerked back awake. Each time I surfaced I looked at the television and realized I was farther downstream in the film's doppelgänger plot—brother and darker brother. They are antithetical twins, good and evil; this is someone else's dream, maybe a group effort. And then I had a dream of my own for what seemed like a moment. I woke confused. In it my father had been away at school, not only for night classes but in residence, as I had been, at college in another city. I wanted to tell him and there he was, literally rising into my field of vision from a crouch, his back breaching the plane of light he stood into. While I slept he had entered the room. He'd lit a tiny goosenecked lamp clamped to a shelf and wrenched it down to shine on the book he was rifling through. His cheek was inscribed with a script of bedclothes, notes from the night school of dream. And he had retrieved something from his dream—a word.

"Dad, what are you doing?"

"Checking a word. In the Czech dictionary."

Checking Czech, hah. A word he had dreamed in an early language of his, the first official language in which he had gone to school, the first in which he had an altered name, before the other names he'd had.

The only glasses he could find were sunglasses, and he had them down over his eyes, with the book sharply angled toward the lamp. He tilted his face up then, a small smile straining with the effort to recall. Where had I seen that face before—a man who cannot see himself for some moments? Wait, it wasn't that I'd seen it—I'd *worn* it, among the chattering speakers of another language, half-aware of wanting my incomprehension to have a pleasant expression. This was a familiar experience for me around my father and would surely be again when I traveled with him. I had to prepare myself to be willing to let words be sounds, music of a sort, as I waited for what would be conveyed to me, what he would translate, and what I could make out for myself. Perhaps it was that idea that made me so unwilling to let that night sound be undeciphered music alone. Even as I sleepily let go of almost everything else, I had still focused on the desire to identify that creature—the sound was an arpeggio of a single note, fanned out slowly, as if thumbed on the tines of a comb. Accurate enough as a description but not yet a proper translation.

For my dad, though, a little breakthrough. Small grunts of negation as he turned a last few pages, swinging one leaf back and forth, and then yes—nearly—yes. He's right, nearly right, just about....

"Yes," he said. "*Panovani.* 'Reign.'"

He looked over at me and tsk-ed. There were pages missing from the dictionary, he said. Not ripped out but unbound to begin with—produced under the communists, of course. Surprising, the force of disappointment in his voice, even though he had found his word, as if the missing pages held a different word he might also need to recover, one that might win a stranger over, even beyond the deception at a border crossing. For my father, charm was more than the practical matter of survival. True safety lay in the winning of regard, the genuine interest a stranger might have for him.

And then for me a recognition, as I too arrive at a moment of definition. That creature's sound. The facts I would confirm later, that it was a small frog I'd been hearing, from a pond a few blocks away (Lakeside was the name of my parents' street). The sound had reverb to it but also the echoey clack underwater from the first summer I could submerge, when, at summer camp, my bunkmates and I would signal to each other by banging rocks together beneath the surface of the lake.

I was only at the camp because my father taught tennis in the summer after he began teaching languages at public school. And he had managed to get us out of the city even before that, on trips full of sudden, approximate identifications. *Look*, he would say, pointing at a shack near Pottersville, *do you see that house? That's like the hut I was born in, but we had straw roofs. Do you see those hills? The same as when I was a boy.* We would have been on the way north, through rolling hills of the Catskills, in the late 1950s and early '60s. At the time, he could not go back to see the originals, the foothills of the Carpathians. It wasn't just the money. He had the teaching work he'd always wanted and some financial stability. But Munkacs was then in the Ukraine and the Soviets did not allow visitors, for military reasons, they claimed. There had been a munitions plant there, and a radar facility had been placed nearby.

The maps were one strand of my preparation for the journey. I also wanted to know as much as I could about the background to the times and places of my father's past. I had spent much of my life hearing his stories and researching the Holocaust, but there was so much to know, and new details emerging continuously, especially since the communist governments of Eastern Europe had fallen and archives long closed were finally accessible.

In all things associated with Holocaust I relied for historical guidance on one of my oldest friends, David Marwell, historian and then head of the Museum of Jewish Heritage in Manhattan's Battery Park. I wasn't alone in this reliance—he is a renowned expert, a historian and ex–Justice Department Nazi hunter who'd been dispatched to Brazil for the examination of Mengele's bones. He had run the Berlin Documents Center, in charge of its archive of Nazi personnel records for six years, and had worked for the National Holocaust Museum. Coincidentally, during my week in New

York, his museum had mounted an exhibition about Jews in Hungarian forced-labor camps, relevant to my father's and Uncle Harry's experiences. It would be helpful see the exhibition and touch base with David while I was there.

The museum exhibit covered history that wasn't new to me. Its photos and installations detailed how Hungary had allied with Nazi Germany in 1938, receiving its piece of Czechoslovakia and embracing Nazi ideas and legal measures against Jews. With the annexation, my Czech father, uncle, and whole paternal family became citizens of Hungary, second class and soon to be much worse. "Citizens Betrayed" was the title of the exhibit, which unfolded in stages the betrayal of the Jews, which had been aided by long-established anti-Semitism. Jewish men eighteen and older were pressed into service not as soldiers (they were labeled unreliable and unfit) but as laborers, though still under military control. The work was demeaning, hard, but bearable at first, though conditions varied according to the attitude of the local commanders. When war was officially declared and Hungary joined the German axis, conditions became harsher; within a year, as Germany attacked the Soviet Union, thousands of ill-equipped Jews were assigned to slave-labor camps or sent as expendables to the Russian front. Easy targets for the cruelty of their own troops, forced to wear yellow armbands, they dug trenches, set explosives, and swept for mines, often without essential training and with no equipment but themselves and their footsteps.

The peculiarities of the Holocaust in Hungary, particularly with regard to these labor battalions, were complex, and individual experience varied greatly depending on location and the character of those in charge. My uncle Harry was sent to the front. My dad, who was working in a bike shop in Budapest at the beginning of the war, would end up in Csepel, a labor camp attached to a Budapest factory. But Harry went first. My dad, still at liberty, found some boots to send Harry and stuffed them with a salami (at this point, even forced laborers could receive packages in the post). Both boots and food were a desperate necessity, though Harry trailed a stink of salami for days afterward. They laughed about it for years.

There was little to laugh about at the time; this was 1942–3, though Harry was in a privileged position in his battalion, a skillful tailor among officers who valued his work on their uniforms. He had even been furloughed to return to Munkacs for a wedding at a time when other Jews were being gassed in the death camps and shot, in their thousands, near where he was stationed. When he missed his return train and reported back late, he was beaten and reassigned to the hardest physical labor. After weeks of searching for mines and digging fortifications, he despaired and attempted suicide by climbing a tall tree and throwing himself from the top. Branches broke his fall, and he only broke his arm. He was sent to the dispensary and missed a fatal culling of the laborers.

So, chance and luck operated in those years. As I worked through the New York exhibit, I stopped at a picture of a man in a distinctive Hungarian army cap, which called to mind another story of my uncle's. In the winter of 1944, Harry wore just such a cap—he had no proper uniform, but the cap was warm and it was so cold in the Ukraine. Yet keeping it on nearly got him killed. Already the Hungarian overseers had abandoned the Jewish workers, fleeing for their lives as the Russians advanced. One day, wandering the no-man's-land this abandonment had created, Harry heard a Russian tank spraying bullets as it crested a hill. He ducked into a ravine. When the firing stopped, Harry jumped up, waving wildly, pointing at himself and shouting in Russian, "A Jew, a Jew!" A head popped out of the tank turret and said in Russian, "*Da, ya znayu*"—"Yes, I know." Then, in Yiddish, "I know because I can count all your bones. But that hat, that soldier's hat…we were about to shoot you. Get rid of it."

My father had a similar end-of-war story, one of many insanely close calls. After he'd escaped from his forced-labor camp and was in hiding, he too met advancing Soviet troops, though the faces of the soldiers who suddenly surrounded him were Asian, Uzbeki troops advancing on Budapest and hunting out enemy soldiers and collaborators. Though he also protested that he was a Jew, the soldiers did not understand and were kicking him and raising bayonets when their commander, a Captain Weinstein, appeared and stayed their guns. *Du bist yets a Yid?* the captain asked in Yiddish—"Are you really a Jew?"—giving my father one of his earliest opportunities to tell his story, the conclusion of which was still highly uncertain.

I finished reviewing the exhibit and headed to David's office. His receptionist waved me in. To come upon someone you've known for thirty years is to see in his face all the faces of his you've ever seen. Before me was the most distinguished version, gray in his full head of hair, though in his eyes, under impressive dark brows, was still the hint of playfulness of the twenty-year-old I had first met. With his characteristic up-from-under look, head slightly bent, he smiled me in. Already on his desk were books relevant to some pressing questions about the route of trains from Munkacs to Auschwitz.

We looked over a map in Gilbert's *Atlas of the Holocaust*. Its arrows were confusing, and we were unsure whether the deportations were from the south or east. So we checked the Auschwitz Kalendarium and some German-language maps. But even with my aunt Lilly's certainty about the date and the thoroughness of the German records of the death trains, we could find no indication of the route for the train Lilly and Shmuel were on. And the maps still seemed to be indicating two possible ways the trains might go.

The Scarecrow's words from *The Wizard of Oz* occurred to me, and I said, "That way is a very nice way. It's pleasant down that way, too. Of course, people do go both ways." I laughed, harder than I should have, harder than the joke warranted. And what Holocaust joke is warranted in the first place? David suggested it might be impossible to know. And that, I replied, is supposed to make me feel better? And we both laughed.

David directed me to some other sources, including the National Archives, where I could find aerial photographs and film of the area taken by pilots on strafing runs or reconnaissance flights. But with the trip now just a few days away, it was becoming apparent that finding the site of Shmuel's death, if possible at all, would require on-the-ground investigation. And luck.

The Friday before our Sunday departure, synagogue services loomed. My father had become something of a daily communicant, and the early morning *minyan* that relied on him was a badge of honor. People knew they could come to Beth El for the requisite eleven months and discharge their duty to their beloved dead by praying the Mourners' Kaddish in a group of at least ten congregants. Of course, he went to synagogue on all the holidays, high and low, for hours at a time, as well as each Friday evening to welcome the Sabbath Queen, Saturday to attend her and hear the Torah read, and back Saturday night to bid her farewell—from the first of the candles to the last whiff of the spice box. He taught at the Sunday school too. He might have snuck off for some golf or tennis on Saturday afternoon (he certainly had in the past), but all this worship made me wonder if even that serious bit of fun was over with. Unkindly, I told him it looked like he was cramming for his finals.

I knew my father wanted me with him at both Friday and Saturday services. Apostate that I was, I offered a sort of unholy trade. I would go on Friday if I could dodge Saturday. I saw his disappointment at once— bringing the out-of-town son to services was important to him, and certainly the full Saturday would be better, with more of the congregation— so I reversed the deal: I would be there on Saturday. I was also aware that he was making a compromise for me by agreeing to travel on Shavuot, a holiday celebrating the giving of the Torah. So I reciprocated.

My mother, who seldom—if ever—went to synagogue with him, had been encouraging me to join him by making hand gestures from the doorway behind him and mouthing "go, go." It was a familiar moment, a miniature version of her vehement encouragement of larger acts of devotion, such as the trip itself. During my time of uncertainty about the trip, she had been plain with me over the phone: *Your father has asked, why are you hesitating? Why haven't you agreed already? Don't you know he wants you to go?* Her cultivated accent, any hint of Brooklyn excised, occasionally forayed into Yiddish: *gut shtikilach brod*—a good piece of bread, as she'd encouraged the cat to be, a solid fellow, reliable. That's what I should be, would be, at agreeing to go. A mensch.

She hadn't minded not being included. She had been to Munkacs on their 1991 trip, when my dad made the pilgrimage to his recently moved mother's grave. My mother had seen the sites that she had helped him speak about in English, the settings for the stories she had made room for him to tell, had prompted him to tell. She had been first to travel as his helpmeet in testimony and witness. I was the one who had to go now. I was the son, an only son, and he very much wanted me to go and to *want* to go.

I wouldn't tell her there was no question of her coming along, had she expressed the desire to. Or rather, it was a question that had never been seriously considered. It was my father who dismissed it as a possibility before it was raised. The issue wasn't just that she would hate the primitive conditions that were inevitable in the Ukraine and would make her disapproval persistently clear. The pitch of her emotional response to any-thing associated with the Holocaust, and also communism—wild grief for the former, furious indignation with the latter—made her presence a potential embarrassment to him. Her politics had long revolved around her perception that the left had abandoned Jews and Israel, but more recently she displayed a new level of general disinhibition, the extent of which had begun to abash anyone connected with her. She had become a vocal and indiscriminate patriot, a neocon klaxon. She'd completed a conversion from liberal Democrat to jingoistic Republican, and her outbursts seemed at times like a species of madness. (A few years later, it would appear that her compulsive behavior might well have been an early and subtle onset of dementia.)

After reading long into Friday night, I found it hard to rise to my fa-ther's morning call to prayer, especially as we might easily have spent an-other hour in bed. We would be un-Jewishly early to services. My father allowed himself the latitude of driving to the synagogue, permissible in his Conservative temple. Predictably among the first, we watched others dribble in as we donned prayer shawls and skullcaps (mine borrowed from the closet at the entrance to the sanctuary). My dad wore an embroidered pillbox-style yarmulke but stuck to the smaller sort of prayer shawl, cover-ing only his shoulders, I was glad to see. The kind that blanketed the whole torso seemed showy to me, unfamiliar anyway. I was stylistically strict if religiously lax in every other way.

I could follow most of the Hebrew of the service, though my late night had me nearly nodding off during the parts where people murmured through the prayers at more or less their own pace, until called back to resume the Jewish version of call and response. I looked forward to the Torah portion, until I realized it would be *Bamidbar*, which translates as "in the wilderness" or "in the desert" but is more familiar as "Numbers." And numbers it is. I love the beauty of the cantillation, the *hazzan's* chant-ing of the portion, but there is no disguising the repetitiveness of the text, reminiscent of the endless begats of Genesis. This isn't genealogy, though, but census, an accounting of the Children of Israel a year out of Egypt, post–golden calf. I consulted the translation in a *chumash* in the pew. The fighting men among them were enumerated under the tribal captains, who were mentioned by name. The Levites were not to be counted among the warriors. They had other duties. The twelve tribes were ranged out along the landscape.

> *The Lord spoke to Moses and Aaron, saying: The Israelites shall camp each with his standard, under the banners of their ancestral house; they shall camp around the Tent of Meeting at a distance. Camped on the front, or east side: the standard of the division of Judah, troop by troop. Chieftain of the Judites: Nahshon son of Amminadab. His troop, as enrolled: 74,600. Camping next to it: The tribe of Issachar. Chieftain of the Issacharites: Nethanel son of Zuar. His troop, as enrolled: 54,400.*

And on and on. They were mustering for the years in the desert. The rabbi attempted to supply some context in his sermon and some meaning for it all. He stressed the relation between the enumeration of the hosts, the tribes, the clans, and the identification of individuals. God discerned the individual in all the numbers, saw them, knew them. And I found myself following along somehow, relating it to the journey we would start the next day. We were in fact ourselves trying to discern, among the numbers, the six million, an individual, Shmuel Steinberger. I suppose, too, I'd been seeing him as some sort of captain, at least potentially. He would have been a leader. And then I caught myself. What was I doing? Was this some kind of divination I was looking for, a message from the Bible that blessed the endeavor to come, a good omen? No, for me anyway, we were heading out to the old God-abandoned killing fields. We would make our own meaning, such as we could. We would have to.

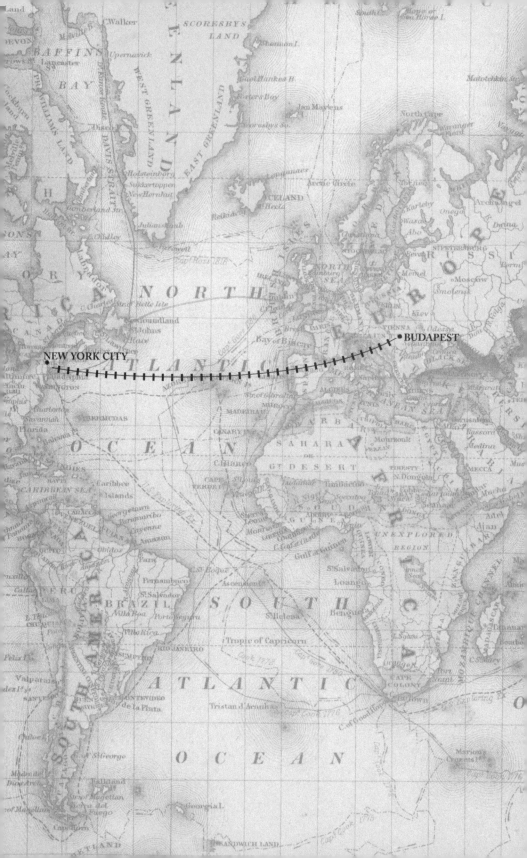

# 5

*My father was an acrobat of stillness*
*once, but only for his own sake, the time*
*he tells about—escaped from labor camp,*

. . . . . . . . . . . . . . . . . . . . . . . . . .

                    *he's penned beneath*
*the stairs of a Budapest apartment house*
*for days, in terror that the least scrape*
*of sound would summon those who'd turn him in—*
*till thirst and hunger drive him to risk the street.*

THE MORNING OF OUR FLIGHT, my dad called Eva Kelenye in Budapest, where it was already evening. He had met Eva during his 1991 trip and stayed in touch since. Jewish and the daughter of a childhood friend of his from Munkacs, she was the source of all things practical for the trip—she owned the apartment we'd be using in Budapest, would be accompanying us to my dad's boyhood home, and had arranged a driver for the journey, the critical journey, from the Ukraine through Slovakia and into Poland. Over the phone, she confirmed details and reminded my dad that when we arrived—Monday morning after our all-night flight—she would be at work. But we had plenty planned for the day of our arrival.

Traveling light, I was determined to pack everything I needed into my carry-on suitcase. An early summer trip meant fewer clothes, which I had selected bearing in mind we would be on the road most of the time, with no access to a washing machine. Nestled among the wash-and-wear pants and shirts was the Sony camcorder I would use to document the trip, along with its additional microphone, lenses, batteries, digital tapes, and the adapters I would need for the variety of countries we'd be passing through. And of course the instructions on how to use this complicated piece of hardware, which required more expertise than I was comfortable with simply to set the date and time. But I had practiced with it before leaving New York, shooting film right up to the night before we left—the footage of my mother and her beloved cat that my father so enjoyed nearly twenty years later.

And then there was my documentation. In a zipper compartment on the soft lid of the bag, its outline visible, was a three-ringed binder with blank paper, some manuscript of my own, and lots of photocopies and printouts: some hole-punched and clipped into the rings, some just slipped into the bulging pockets, front and back, of the binder's cover. They were the maps of the train routes and roads, as well as copies of book pages, including several from the Auschwitz Kalendarium, and three poor reproductions of photographs of Munkacs in the 1930s. There was also a small hardback notebook that would become my diary.

In the cab to Kennedy Airport, my father practiced some Spanish with our Salvadoran driver. I had enough Spanish to follow the conversation well enough, but the exchange reminded me that we were headed to linguistic terrain I would be utterly unable to manage. On the plane, a direct flight on Malév Hungarian Airlines, I was also conscious of the very different cultural context global travel can suddenly plunge us into, and when I took out a small pamphlet from the Museum of Jewish Heritage's Hungarian Labor Battalion exhibit, I felt suddenly self-conscious and buried it quickly among other papers lest I give offense to the Hungarians around me.

Budapest loomed large in my father's wartime experience: as a big city he came to for work as an adolescent in 1942; as the site of his enslavement at a labor camp after the German occupation; and where he reunited with his brother Harry at war's end, learned of the devastation of his family, and began his long journey of displacement. And he had been here since, several times, including a 1972 visit (where he discovered that the communists had changed all the street signs) and his trip with my mother in 1991. So he knew his way around. For myself, I was keen to let him be my guide through this important part of his past, and to map the landscape topography to the landscape of his stories from that time.

*Volodya and Eva, our indispensable guides and helpmates*

That first morning, after leaving our bags at the apartment Eva had arranged for us, he brought me to the area around King Street, as he Englished the name, in search of the first place he had hidden after his escape from the Csepel labor camp in the summer of 1944. He had been abandoned by his fellow escapee, Imre Naiman, and had wandered the city looking for shelter. He hid under a set of stairs in an old apartment building for a week, in fear of any movement, the smallest sound that might give him away. It was the beginning of a harrowing series of hiding places and narrow escapes he would endure for the next year.

But now, over a half century later, my dad wasn't certain which building was the exact one. It might have been here, he said in front of one house. Or maybe that one over there. No, this. And back down the block, and up again. We crossed to the other side of the street. He looked up the buildings, scanned again left and right, and we crossed back. He walked briskly to the left and settled on one, stood at the entrance. Had he had a dowser's pluck of some sort, a flash of memory?

We took advantage of someone exiting and went in. The entryway was

57

arched, with wooden doors within larger wooden panels, together filling the plane of space—designed for carriages originally. It led to an inner courtyard with outer stairways up to the flats, much like the building where we were staying: four stories of terraces around that inner space, with doors to each apartment.

We stood, gazing up. Was this the actual building? Could it be? At the back, directly across from the entrance, was some kind of small business with a service entrance near it. The door was half opened, and we approached it as if on an errand. We had at once, both of us, assumed an air of purpose as a disguise that would allow us to explore and examine without interference. The few people around did not challenge us as we passed through the door, my father leading the way. He seemed to be aware of the geography of the building.

But even I had observed the similarity of these prewar buildings. A few steps in we immediately found a small set of stairs, a flight down with a landing midway and a little farther down a short corridor, staircases going up. It had obvious potential as my dad's hiding place, secreted, untrafficked, with some barrels and boxes that looked like they had been stored for quite a while. Easy to imagine this space as a place to hide. But surely we would just be imagining? I asked my father: "This couldn't be it, could it?"

He was looking intently around him.

"So, it's like where you hid?" I said.

He said nothing but slowly nodded his head; he was far off inside that head for a few moments.

I pressed him: "Like the place—not the place, of course."

"Yes," he says, meaning no.

And so we left. The simulacrum would have to be enough for today. Yet the search and pause and questioning made me think of that place where he had never been but which was the purpose of our trip to identify. The bridge. There would be no room for uncertainty there. No similar structure would do. And when we would arrive at what my painstaking, inconclusive research would tell us *might* be the fateful site of Shmuel's death, we would have no one present whose memory might be jogged. Only stories to guide us, that faultiest form of barely preserved witness; simply testimony, hard won, but passed along through several people, with the inevitable distortions. Yet, for all that, still precious. Because who does not feel the critical importance of holding on to the narratives of those who have died? Some-one would want to know, if there were someone left to want that, someone to whom the lost one was dear, someone who was dear to the lost one.

That first day was a long day, with much to take in. Eva, who'd already told us she would be at work when we arrived, had left us directions to an antifascist organization where she believed we would get some detail about rail routes to Auschwitz. We made our way there by tram, but the organization's staff, while eager to help, told us nothing we didn't already know. As we left their building, I noted with a start that we were on Oktogon Square.

My father had been here in 1945. I had heard the details of that visit from him a number of times, spoken and written. After a long trek through shattered streets, snow-covered and full of the corpses of soldiers and horses, he had entered the square and come upon a crowd clustered around bodies hanging from lampposts. Or rather one already hanging and another being hoisted. There were no gallows, trapdoors, or drops. The two people were being strangled from the cross members of the lamps with thin rope, almost invisible from where he stood. He left after moments, revolted.

I'd first read the story in a letter he had sent from Budapest in 1972, his first time back. It was highly uncharacteristic of his travel correspondence, which tended toward a few highlights and lists of places. But then that had been a first return. He was proud that he could find his way around despite the way the communists had changed the street names, and he couldn't help recalling what he saw that winter, decades before.

I would hear of the incident again on a number of occasions, but not today, on the spot itself. I waited for a surge of memory from him, but he stayed silent on the subject. I wondered at that. This was the first of what would be many places on this trip where, long ago, he'd experienced vio-lence, fear, revulsion. Places I knew from his stories. That I had anticipated seeing. How would he react? What would it lead to between us?

I was accustomed to the sudden strike of memory, his availability to it, but his silence today made me realize how I had to wait—had so of-ten waited, unconsciously—for the past to be invoked when I was around him, especially with other people present. But I saw that, even here, with reminders everywhere, I couldn't be certain when that would happen. It wasn't Proustian, involuntary. It could be resisted, suppressed, or simply deflected by other claims on his attention. If there was to be happiness for him, for anyone who'd had a life like his, his memory often had to be off duty; he had to be fully in the present. Yet despite the unpredictability, his initial silence was a mercy for me as well. I had worried that I was going to be overwhelmed by a constant avalanche of difficult recollection. What comfort could I offer, was I able for? And the worry would persist, for sure, given the central purpose of our trip.

Whatever comfort my dad would find in commemorating his brother, I would have an active part in. That our goal was not solely and exclusively his past offered breathing room—for both of us. And my place, as I saw it, was not simply to wait for the stories to descend, or not. I could, I would, be adding to those stories, supplying detail he might want to know and did not. And I had done some research on Oktogon, beyond the endless examination of railway lines.

He'd assumed the Russians were doing the hanging, on-the-spot summary executions of Arrow Cross men—Hungarian Nazis, put in power when Hitler took charge of his wavering allies. The Russians were, in fact, doing the puppetry, through local communists, and would be for another forty years plus. But I had learned through my research that the situation had been more complicated. There had been a trial the day before, by a newly established "People's Tribunal." I was in a position to tell him who'd been executed and how richly they deserved it. I had the notes.

He had witnessed the execution of Sergeant Rotyis and Corporal Szivos, Hungarians who had murdered 124 members of a Jewish labor battalion. Though the hanging wasn't the first my father had witnessed, it was the first outside his own battalion labor camp, and the justice had perhaps been too swift, the killing too slow. But the victims were the correct ones this time. He would see others, including Germans.

I had wondered at the shock he had expressed in past retellings about German bodies, one young German soldier in particular. He mentioned that young man many times, fair-haired and handsome, as contorted as any of the frozen corpses he'd encountered on his long walk into the city. And the hanging. Always, he spoke of the particular way he had been struck then and there with "man's inhumanity to man." I wanted to relieve that sympathy—mostly because I found it difficult to believe that, having been through what he had, he had sympathy to spare for such as these, even a momentary sort.

Later that day, after a rest at the apartment, my dad brought me to a place he had mentioned many times, an iconic spot in his personal history: the front steps of the Erzsébet School. I had seen a mysterious photo from his 1991 trip with my mother: a snapshot of five steps and a cement balustrade fronting a red-brick column with the address on an oval sign. In a city as complicated as a place could be for him, these steps were a nexus of the most extreme joy and sorrow.

In the summer of 1945, liberated but in flight from the Red Army to avoid forced patriation to the USSR, my dad had come here to find his family. The school housed an office of the National Relief Committee for Deportees, a Jewish organization that assisted survivors in finding each other after the war, collecting information and maintaining a message board. On its steps, he was reunited with his brother Harry—and at the same time learned of those, just as close to him, who didn't make it.

So he took me to this spot of endings and beginnings, of mourning and celebration, of the beginning of the struggle toward a new life. He wanted to see again the steps, and he wanted me to see them too.

I didn't know what to expect, and for a moment I didn't even notice the front stairs, the school structure itself was so imposing—a striking art nouveau building with elaborate columns and brickwork and a Turkish-looking central dome above an undulating roofline. The iconic steps were part of a stairway very modest by comparison with the building's grandeur.

"Dad, the building. It's something."

"Yes, it's beautiful."

"You never mentioned."

He shrugged. "I wasn't looking at the architecture. I was looking for Shmuel, for Harry, for the others."

"Sorry, Dad. Of course."

After more than fifty years, the steps were all that mattered.

"The building *is* beautiful," he said, "but back then you could hardly see the place for the people, crowds up and down. You had to swim through them. People registered inside. Others were out here, waiting. There was a

61

*The steps of what had been the Erzsébet School in Budapest. After the war it was where refugees went to be reunited with family or to seek news. The steps were a place of waiting, and most often of mourning.*

bulletin board inside, with a list of names of survivors they changed every hour, but you had to push in to see."

In my research I had learned that in June of 1945, more than 25,000 people had come to this spot to look for survivors. I said that to my dad.

"That many?"

"You want to go inside?"

He looked at the door and shook his head. "No, no, we shouldn't disturb. And everything happened out here, on the steps and on the street."

He had come here over a period of days that June. On the first day, he scanned the lists on the bulletin board as they were updated. Like everyone. He did not see any of the names he was looking for, but he was learning the dimensions of the catastrophe from the sheer scale of the names *not* included. He made his way outside, pushing through the crowds of those like himself, weeping, speaking together, trying to make sense of the aggregate lost. On the steps that first day he met Chaim, a cart driver from Munkacs, with whom he and Shmuel once hauled wood. He had been a large boisterous man, a jokester, but now he was a bony whisperer who wept in my father's arms and had no news of anyone. He had last seen Shmuel in the Munkacs ghetto.

After my father's recounting of that first reunion, I prompted him: "You had to return several times, right?"

"Three times. I came the next day, and the day after."

He had met Chaim again the next morning, still grieving and waiting on the steps. The number of refugees had diminished somewhat. Nothing for him on the bulletin board. As the fruitless hours passed, he despaired, stood to leave, then heard a woman's voice calling him: Dvora, a friend of his mother's with news of one survivor, his mother's sister, his aunt Irene, who had returned from Auschwitz and had recovered enough to head home, though Dvora didn't know where she was staying. My father never did find her. And though my dad welcomed Dvora's reminiscences of his mother, how bright and lively she had been, the meeting was one of overwhelming sorrow: Dvora's two sons were dead, and her husband likely dead too, though unconfirmed, which was why she had remained at the school. My dad consoled her, despairing himself of ever finding his brothers.

The third morning, inside the building, as he was pushing his way to the bulletin board, a hand touching his shoulder turned him around: a familiar face, Mottel, a trade-school classmate, a fellow mechanic. But why was he so excited? What was he saying?

"Your brother," Mottel said.

"Which?"

"Your brother Harry. I just saw him! Come!"

Mottel yanked him toward the door.

"Run, run," Mottel shouted, and the two of them ran together through the crowd, out the door, and down the steps.

And there was Harry, walking away, a girl with him. It was Lilly. My father's voice failed him. He couldn't make a sound, and it was Mottel who shouted down the street. Harry turned around and the brothers ran for each other, colliding into an embrace that they held and held, by turns crying and laughing.

"Where have you been?" Harry asked, almost reproachfully. "We've been searching for you for months."

They opened their embrace to include Lilly and held each other for a long time. Finally, they disengaged and sat on the steps to share their experiences and relate what they knew of the others. They were there for hours. My father's first thoughts had been for Shmuel, but Harry barraged him with so many questions it was some minutes before Lilly told him, briefly, in summary, what she knew. Then Harry told my dad what he'd heard from Shmuel's friend Zlate Raisel.

I had heard this story many times, of course, but I listened as my father told me these things again, standing in front of the steps that brought the details back to him, the steps that were both an icon for return and recovery but also for understanding the permanence of the losses. I asked some questions I knew the answers to, but I wanted to have the words here, in their original place. If not quite the original words.

"Dad, what language were you and Harry speaking then, Yiddish?"

He looked surprised. "Sure, Yiddish, with my family always and besides I wanted so much to. I couldn't for such a long time. You know I spoke secretly to the horses I took care of when I hid on the farm."

He laughed at himself at this.

"It's just that you and Harry spoke so much Hungarian later on. And another thing: You didn't find out everything at that meeting, right? I mean, you didn't try to tell each other *everything* that happened."

I think he found the question a little strange. And I wasn't quite sure myself what I wanted to know.

He said, "Well, we told quickly where we had been and generally what happened. We were going to be together then."

"There would be time to talk."

"Yes, but later and little by little. But he and Lilly did tell me they were getting married in a few days. A *simcha*, at last something to be joyful about."

"Lilly, did she talk then, or afterward?"

"Lilly told us about Auschwitz but not much. We heard a lot from others. She said about her father and her brothers, her family. We all went over who we knew—who we knew were gone."

"And Shmuel?"

The template, the story from the time that now would guide us on our twenty-first-century journey, was from Zlate Raisel. An Auschwitz survivor, she had made sure to be in the same freight car as he was. Lilly had been elsewhere on that train and, like Harry, would hear of Shmuel's fate after liberation, back in Munkacs. Harry and Lilly had returned to await the others of their family who would never return. But they had found each other and Zlate Raisel, who had news.

She and Shmuel had been together as much as they could manage after the Nazis created ghettos in Munkacs in April 1944, in preparation for deportation. They had been in a relationship for about three years; not quite a forbidden love but not one to be encouraged, either, which might well have provided an added intensity. She was his girlfriend and also his niece, the daughter of a half-sister, Sarel, one of the seven children of my grandfather's first marriage.

Shmuel was seventeen. The transport left on the morning of May 19, 1944, from a makeshift ghetto—sheds and open spaces—in a brickyard close to the Latorice River. The journey would last three days. Shmuel had raised the idea of escape fairly early, causing a long, ongoing argument in the car. Their treatment was bad enough not to encourage expectation of anything better to follow. The conditions in the car were abysmal: no food or water, air fetid with the stench of waste from a bucket and the odors of frightened humanity. The mass was packed together so tightly that the dead were held upright for days. Zlate did not need to concentrate on those things in the telling. Harry knew already—from Lilly, from others—and he would hear much more when he went to Budapest, desperately searching for his other brother, or for news.

Zlate had argued with Shmuel, begging him not to do anything foolish. In turn, he tried to persuade her that *not* to do anything would be foolish. He spoke about somehow getting out of the boxcar and escaping, the pair of them. He, at least, wanted to fight, to join the Russians to the east and kill those who murder Jews. She was sure they would be killed in the attempt. But he could say with good reason that she ought to see the trajectory otherwise—how could she not?—the beatings and starvation of the ghetto, the killings to this point, and now this train car.

He pushed his way to the window with her and began working at the barbed wire that covered the rectangular opening. Other voices protested, taking her side, fearful of what he was doing, that he would be observed, that he would bring even more trouble on them all. He had to stop at times, interrupted by the halts on sidings and stations, soldiers around stretching their legs, passing their car. There was time spent just holding Zlate, quietly, and more discussion, remonstration. But on and off he persisted, mostly with his bare hands, wrapping the wire with cloth as he pulled on it, gouging with an implement, maybe a spoon—utensils were precious and closely kept—until he could move the wire aside. Then he waited for his chance.

It came with a river bridge. The journey was nearly over, which he would have anticipated, and he must have expended considerable effort getting out of the high window of the Karlsruhe freight car, about five feet up. How had he been able to hang, so as to fling himself out and down into the river? What river? He'd begun to swim across to a shore. The train had stopped meanwhile, backed up. The shooting started as soon they got him in their sights. Soldiers dismounted and pursued him; more gunfire. And then the shooting stopped. He died in a field by a river near a bridge.

According to Zlate, Shmuel was killed several hours before the train reached the ramp at Auschwitz-Birkenau. Could this help us find that bridge? How far away that made the site from the camp was difficult to say from her approximation, even if her time sense was accurate in the midst of her shock and grief. So many variables had to be considered were we to find the actual place. True, rate times time equals distance, but the rate was cruelly disrupted, which had greatly magnified time, the three days taken to go a modest distance. The 419 kilometers—around 260 miles—by road from Munkacs to Auschwitz through Slovakia would be about six hours at a straight drive. The track adds miles, hard to say exactly how many with all the curves, often following the banks of the rivers rather than crossing them, and that should have taken, as it still would today, about twelve hours.

The more northerly Polish corridor, longer, would have meant an additional eight hours of travel. But I had found no reference to that route, though I never quite freed myself of the fear of discovering that some rare chance had taken this one transport that way. Perhaps topography had slowed them in places. But how had they been three days and two nights, seventy-two hours, on the rails? Where were the delays—how long had they been? All those things could never be known with any certainty. There could be no more clues from Zlate Raisel, who had died in a car accident in Israel a decade before the trip. We could compensate somewhat for the unknowns by widening the area of our search. And the time was fast approaching when all this speculation, this uncertainty, would have to be resolved. Or not.

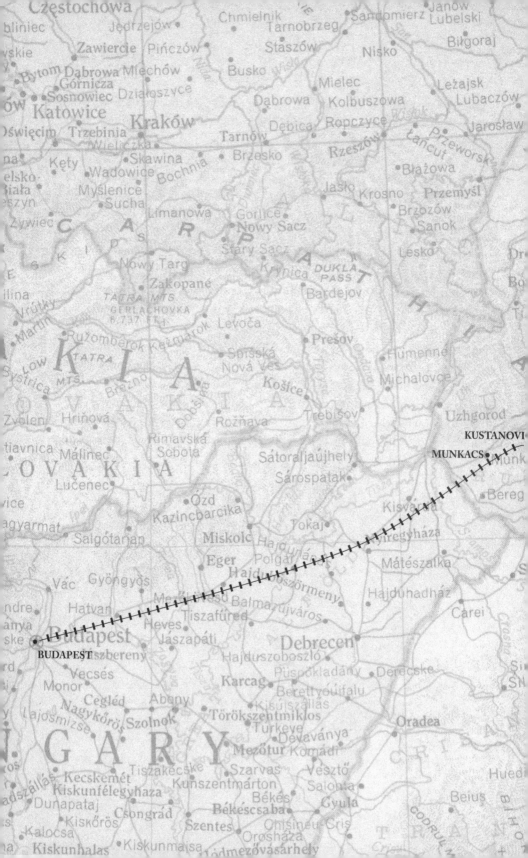

# 6

*I'm nowhere then,*
*abstracting his story out of its settings,*
*wanting to think of it as a large stone,*
*a boulder under which are things I need.*
*The straw-roofed Czech village, and the camps*
*with the strung wire through which the dark eyes plead*
*like droning whole notes on a musical staff,*
*a diagram of sorrow, are a stone*
*which I, a Theseus, putting off majority,*
*can't lift.*

OUR TRAIN TO MUNKACS LEFT BUDAPEST EARLY—painfully early for me, after a fitful night of sleep, dreaming of other tracks, other routes. Munkacs had been the starting point of so many dreadful rail journeys, Shmuel's among them. But we were also bound for the starting point in another sense—headed for the original places, the beginnings of the family I had heard most about: my grandmother, Yitta Feiga; her children Herschel, Yehuda Melech (who became Jay in the United States), and Shmuel—Shmiel. And for ten or so miserable years my grandfather had been with them, Moses Eliahu, full of drink and rage, a nominal Hasid. A family whose life had begun and continued in extreme poverty, first in the village of Kustanovice, with its handful of Jews, and then in Munkacs, whose substantial Jewish population made up about half the city and supported a large yeshiva.

Eva, who would accompany us, met us at the station with a suitcase laden with gifts for her friends and family back home. We were in good hands. Her deep blue eyes were a fitting indicator of her energy and intentness. She always appeared alert and able to summon her force, her competence, for whatever was at hand: giving directions in Budapest or organizing something or other on the phone. I often had no idea what she was saying, but the tone was definite, well organized, and warm. There was a quality nevertheless of containment. There was nothing nervous about her—no fidgetiness—just repose in readiness and then right into motion for however long it was required.

As the great plain of Hungary monotonously slipped past, I pulled out my stash of papers, glanced at a map, but quickly turned to my photocopies of Roman Vishniac's pictures of Munkacs in the 1930s. Culled from his book *A Vanished World*, these black-and-white photographs had been a compelling visual template of my father's city from the moment I saw them. What Vishniac had done for Munkacs, Mukachevo—what he had done for Jewish Eastern Europe at large—would persist in me as it had for many others. These photos truly became my map of the city. They presented scenes so vivid I felt I knew Munkacs before I set a foot in it. They were aids to imagination and at the same time one thing less that I had to imagine. And they allowed me a little closer to my father, to where he had come from. A small way of joining the story.

My dad had so often tried to show my mother and me approximations of his old-country origins that it was a family joke. Anywhere we went, especially car trips outside the city, could become a chance to point out resemblances. As an adolescent, when his past felt like an imposition on the here and now, my joking sometimes had a mean streak to it. Never a joke to me, however, was that he had no photograph of his mother, or his efforts to collect the features of her from the faces of the world—actresses on television, billboard and magazine photographs. So when Vishniac's book was published, I bought it for him immediately. Not that I anticipated the miraculous possibility of finding his mother in the background of some scene, but I hoped he would recognize someone. Since leaving college I had lived in places far from my parents, and sending them pictures of my children, though a meager substitute for presence, was something. How would it be never to have those reminders of the presence that had been?

So perhaps Vishniac's images would bring my dad nearer to what he wanted to find. For years, I had wondered whether it was for himself he needed to search out these approximations of his past, or more to show them to us. Sometimes I believed he wanted to increase our appreciation of how far he had come, as encouragement to devote more of our love in compensation for all the losses. Other times he seemed to be musing aloud, and we were overhearing his own amazement at his survival, at his eventual thriving. And such long odds—almost no one pictured in the Vishniac book had survived.

Looking now at these photocopies, I thought back to the day in 1983 when I arrived with *A Vanished World* at my parents' new house. It was a time of crowning achievement for my dad: the house in the suburbs that he and my mother had always coveted; being named National Teacher

*Dad being honored by President Ronald Reagan in 1983 for his work on the National Commission for Excellence in Education*

of the Year and serving on President Reagan's "Excellence in Education" commission; a Rose Garden ceremony for him at the White House, hosted by Nancy Reagan; a series of public occasions where he was introduced as survivor, refugee, and an embodiment of the famous dream fulfilled. Television interviews and speeches. While warning of the crisis in American education, he had offered himself as an example of America's promise kept, all true in that sum and summary way, in ringing generalities.

I was on my own journey, which had taken me from Ireland to Massachusetts to Missouri. After my long history of approach-avoidance with my dad, the solo visit from St. Louis with the Vishniac book was a gesture of sorts. I was hardly in the door before laying the big book ceremoniously on the dining room table and arranging my parents around it. Anxious that it yield something, I had bookmarked every Munkacs photo. I stooped behind them as Dad paged through.

The first figures of his first city were Meshorerim singers—Hasidic choristers of the "court" of Rabbi Baruch Rabinowitz, followed by children in *payos*—sidelocks—studying the Talmud. After shots of some "ordinary" Jews, we were returned to Rabinowitz's court: two interiors of Hasidim at study.

"Your father was Hasidic, wasn't he?" I said.

"Yes, he wore the clothes, the long coat, and we had to have *payos*, the three boys. But he wasn't really religious."

"A drinker, right?"

"Well, yes."

"Which *rebbe* did he follow, or say he did?"

He considered a moment. "I don't know."

It was understandable that he didn't. He had avoided his father because when the man was unavoidable, it was often painful, even dangerous.

We resumed with more candids of religious figures: paired elders, rabbi and sexton according to Vishniac, homeward bound after morning prayers, elongated shadows leading the way; two out-of-town yeshiva boys; worshippers departing the main synagogue; more street boys. Still no face for him to light on among the faces. He passed over them without remarking until plate 123, when he paused, with a little start, staring at the large photo: two men walking toward the camera on a rain-glossed street. The caption referred to a "fool."

The bearded man with a handkerchief on his head was not the fool. Assisted by a cane, he was described as a "wealthy citizen of Mukachevo" who was protecting his fur hat from the rain and bringing the fool home to dinner. According to Vishniac, neighbors in "every Jewish community" took turns caring for the mentally challenged.

My father clicked his tongue, pointing to the man on the right. I gave him a little time and tried to be calm.

"You knew him?"

"Yes, poor soul, a retarded man. He would walk around the streets."

I couldn't help thinking of how quickly he would have been selected for the gas—how the Germans "practiced" Holocaust in 1940 on the disabled. But even had he made it to the ramps, he would not have been one of those selected for work. With the Hungarian Jews, there was a rush to slaughter.

"What's his name?" I asked.

"Such a sweet face," my mother said. "And look at how he has his hands in the opposite sleeves."

"Like a muff," I said.

"A muff?" my father asked.

"Oh, you know, Judah," my mother said, "the tube women used, instead of gloves, fur-lined sometimes."

And there was a hint of the feminine about this man: his heavyset companion walked, one foot before the other, but the so-called fool's feet were parallel. He must have been shuffling.

"Dad, his name?"

"Meyer Tsits we called him."

"Where are they? I mean in Munkacs?" I felt a strong impulse to locate them on the streets, particularly in relation to others, to my father himself, his mother, his brothers. The photograph must have been taken in the late afternoon. My grandmother would have been laundering clothes in someone's basement; my dad, fourteen and already apprenticed, welding in the bike shop.

"Do you remember the name of street?" I asked.

"Bokko Corso," my father said, "maybe near Kertvarosh."

If we made the photograph ground zero and imagined we were in Munkacs, how close would these men be to the cellar my father's family lived in, without his father by then—and in what direction? Would they be near the schoolyard or off in another direction, toward the pond? An odd thought, to superimpose that world on this, to join them. Not the first time I had it, though.

Meyer Tsits. Tsits was "tits" in Yiddish, wasn't it? One word I did know. I asked my dad about that.

"Children used to tease him with that."

"How, tease?" I asked. Looking again at Meyer.

"They would shout, the boys, 'Your mother has breasts.' And he went meshuga, chasing after, down the street, yelling, with spit coming out his mouth."

"So, you teased him?"

"No, never."

"Really?"

"Yes," he said, about to turn the page.

I delayed him with questions—that sign on the wall behind them, "Mydlow," what does it mean? How old was Meyer? I held him back because I didn't believe him. I wanted to give him a chance to change his answer, to elaborate. But he didn't. The page turned. I didn't believe that he alone of all the local boys was never cruel to Meyer Tsits.

More than that, suddenly, desperately, I wanted him to ask forgiveness of Meyer. I wanted him to need forgiveness of someone, to be responsible for even a minor wrong, and own up—surely not a wrong of the sort connected with camps and killing squads, but some small act he might have done and regretted. Then I could ask forgiveness too, of him, for doubting so many ordinary things he said, and he might ask forgiveness of me, too. We might forgive each other, as needed, and say what we were forgiving. It would be possible then to have a language in common in which we could say these things aloud, and maybe what we would speak of would not have to do with the largest of matters—the terrible suffering and death—and would just be about the things between us, matters between fathers and sons.

He turned to a picture of an entryway—stairs behind wrought iron railings, crowded with Hasidim.

"Is this near where Meyer walked, Dad?"

"Not far, back in the direction they came from."

Another picture brought us inside. The Hasidim argue there in pairs, contesting to find the truth in the word, of the Talmud, of the sages, and all of them—the dead sages and living scholars—seeking to understand the revealed word. They are certain of the truth in the words. They have only to discover it. They believe in the world to come, the Hasidim. They talk about it in ways that other sorts of Jews do not. They believe in the immortality of the soul. I knew this because I, full of collegiate certainty, had disputed with my father when he mentioned that as an article of faith for Hasidim. I said that Jews don't trouble about those sorts of things, even the Orthodox. But, no, they did, he'd told me, and he was right. I hadn't yet done any investigation. He knew; he'd lived among them. I could be relied on to check details in books, but this was his life we were looking into.

So we gazed together at these ironclad believers in caftans, homburgs—*kippahs*. Even in the old-seeming world of black-and-white photographs, they dressed like citizens from another, older world. I thought of their concern with yet another world again, the world to come, which they call Gan Eden, Eden, Paradise, the garden before time that would be after time too. If Meyer Tsits had kept the law and loved his God, he would be in Paradise. And maybe there he could forgive, would have done so already, understood what forgiveness was. For to ask forgiveness of Meyer Tsits in this world is to imagine him, for an instant of belief as long as a shutter's click, as he never was.

I began to give in to the rhythm of the train and, returning the pictures to my backpack, allowed myself to doze. Suddenly there were uniforms in the car asking for passports. We were at the Ukrainian border. I looked across at my father and he was serious, and stiff. I felt a chill, another moment of resonance, and then immediately the absurdity of the chill—all those films, those fictions, desperate escapees with forged papers. Truly silly and maybe worse, a self-indulgence, a Holocaust frisson. And I had some real fears—about what lay ahead, concerning my responses. Would I be able to comfort my father? Would my own resentments get in the way? Still, even the name of the border town, Chop, evoked something. After a pretty river crossing—the Tisza—and more guards, we were there, a town name I'd seen in connection to the route of deportations. But had it been Shmuel's route to Auschwitz? The Allies, fully informed, had been entreated to bomb this rail yard to save the Hungarian Jews from the annihilation unfolding during those eight weeks in 1944. The Allies didn't bomb.

Another hour and we were in Munkacs. Right off the train, our driver, Volodya, greeted us—and I was introduced. I was a bit taken aback at first: the steely gray mustache and hair reminded me of Stalin, and he spoke Russian in an emphatic style that suggested anger where there was none. As we walked out of the station, Eva filled me in a little, in her halting English. I hadn't realized that my father knew him, from his trip in 1991. I was struck, not for the first time, with my dimness about things. I followed along, a step behind in understanding—resigned and consigned—monolingual among the polyglots but also uncertain of my reactions, sure that some would be unacceptable.

I was pleased to learn that Volodya was a hydroelectric engineer, responsible for this area of the Ukraine and with extensive knowledge of the rivers of the region. His expertise would be useful. But I was also a little annoyed. If my father had thought to mention it, he might have saved me some hours of inconclusive research about river levels throughout the area. (Though I learned later that changes since the war had been negligible, more to do with the seasons than larger shifts in climate.)

We emerged from the train station onto the cobbles of a sort of square, if a curvy one—an open convergence of streets: Vokzalna, Yaroslava Mudroho on one side; Luchkaia on the other. The street signs were on the sides of buildings, as in Hungary, but in Cyrillic. I could barely make them out, but the shock of semi-illiteracy had been blunted by the days in Budapest. Hungarian had been impenetrable to the ear, certainly, and pretty much to the eye too, despite its Roman script. And I had done some preparation for the Ukraine, at least with the alphabet. I should have prepared for the car as well—a venerable, beaten-up Lada, vintage circa late seventies. Perhaps seeing my dubious gaze, Volodya smiled and said, "OK, mechanic." By which I took it that the car was all right mechanically—though it may have referred to his own skill in keeping it that way. Dad greeted Volodya warmly and they fell into conversation in Russian. I heard Mukachevo. I heard Kustanovice. The itinerary, no doubt.

Before me was Munkacs in color. I half expected the monochrome of the Vishniac photographs, but Munkacs favors pastel. Now and in the past, according to the others in the car with me. Salmon and pale yellows

*My father and I at the grave of my grandmother, Yitta Feiga, in the "New Jewish Cemetery,"
Koropets, outside of Munkacs. She is buried under her maiden name, Muller.*

dominated, and some tan. The neat cobblestones continued on many of
the roads. Our first destination would take us east out of town, to the New
Jewish Cemetery and my grandmother's grave. At Eva's instigation, we
traversed the city through the center, so I could see something of it. It had
a pedestrian area, which we slowly skirted, and as we swung past I caught
a glimpse of a building with a clock tower, city hall in mint green—one of
the favored postcard images of Munkacs along with Palanok Castle, which
loomed on its hill to the west. Near here was the old Jewish section, several
sites in fact, to which we would return later.

Meyer Tsits was on my mind. And Lilly, too: Meyer's street scene was out
of Vishniac. Hers I had first from her own descriptions of being marched
to the brickworks and the trains, driven out of the ghetto, past the theater,
wherever those places were exactly, behind us now as we headed east. Some
time ago—after hearing Lilly's description—I would see a photograph of
one of those scenes, a group of Munkacs Jews forced down the street on that
march ahead of the transports. And now here I was, so near that spot.

The city's edge, and beyond, was quickly identifiable by the roads, ill-maintained, even rutted, especially these secondary ones. The cemetery also looked unkempt. We parked roadside and Dad led the way, tramping through long grass. The grave was close to a mausoleum, with impressive headstones of Hasidic rabbis and family visible within, which made my grandmother's plot easy to find.

We followed to the stone. This was the grave. In Hebrew lettering: Feiga Muller, her maiden name. We collected pebbles to place on the monument, as the custom is, a record of visitors showing respect. My father insisted we take a series of images—me with him, the marker between us, him alone. As I stood there, with Volodya behind the camera, I couldn't help recalling how much uneasiness there had been at the transfer of the grave ten years earlier. I had the reports from my mother of the difficulties, the anxious transatlantic phone calls. People had to be trusted. People had to be paid in a roundabout sort of way—goods gotten to them that they could sell. Arrangements had been elaborate, but the unease had been put to rest somehow. The sons had done their duty. They had to believe the Ukrainians, Jews among them—one distant relative—had done theirs. I wondered again whether there could be any escape from the approximations, any way to go beyond what amounted to faith. I thought of that other grave, if there was one, the unhallowed ground, a field by a river, a railroad bridge.

Dad asked for some time alone by the grave, so the rest of us walked to the car. We were to continue east from here to Kustanovice, the village of his birth, the place where whatever my father had to sustain him was given, by Feiga. Now was my chance to talk to Volodya about the train route. I had waited uneasily, and I wasn't sure how to make myself clear. He really had very little English, and I didn't want my father in the middle as translator. My continuing uncertainty reflected on my competence, I felt. I grabbed a map out of my backpack. I should have been sure by now, should have searched out every source. To be fair—to myself—I had located quite a few, had a good deal of evidence, and certainty was a fantasy. Still, I needed to know from Volodya, or to decide with him, which way we would be setting out from Munkacs. I beckoned him to join me by the hood of the car, where I unfolded the map.

I leaned over the paper, to shade it from the bright sun, and tried to point out the minuscule lines that indicated railway tracks. He nodded.

Then I traced the way north first, up through Poland, and looked up at him, pausing a second. Then went back down to the map and traced the route through Slovakia. I looked up and shrugged.

He shook his head vigorously, "*Nyet nyet nyet.*"

Which route was he *nyetting?*

"*Da?*" I asked, making it a question and pointing again at the lines through Slovakia.

"Ah," he said, "*momyent.*"

He went back to the car and pulled out a paper of his own. It was a printout, an internet map of Slovakia and a small part of Poland with a single rail route highlighted in yellow marker. The Slovakia route.

"Are you sure? How do you know?" I said to him, in English. He looked at me. Puzzled, of course. True—what was the Russian word for "true"? *Pravda,* right? That famously untruthful newspaper?

"*Pravda?*" I said.

He looked at me for a moment, laughed, and called to my dad, who was walking toward us. I could tell he had been crying but he seemed all right, even energetic.

"Jay, Jay," Volodya said, loosing a torrent of Russian, out of which I recognized Slovakia—and a town name or two, including Chop, which I now learned I had been pronouncing incorrectly. It is a long "o."

"He says we will follow through Slovakia. That that's the way, as best we can, that we have a car and not marching like an army. We will do what we can do."

"But how does he know that's the way they took, the transports?"

My father translated the question and the answer, which came with a shrug to him and a nod to me.

We knew; everybody knows.

What they knew accords with other evidence, with documents, with the testimony of survivors. In the villages and towns along the way, the people knew which way the Jews went, and their children know now, and grandchildren. They simply knew. Still know.

"So, Dad, now Kustanovice?"

We would talk about Shmuel there, I was sure. I would ask about him, for one thing, but I could tell we were still very much within the bounds of my father's own story, his recollections of himself in these places, and this

79

part of our trip would be haunted by his love of loves and grief of griefs: his mother.

We got into the car and set off on an occasionally bone-jarring ride, one small road to another. My father had a little exchange with Volodya, and after a little while we pulled up to a building with a pebble-dash surface and a corrugated metal roof—not a house, not a hut—with a few outbuildings.

"What's this?" I asked.

The place looked nothing like the Kustanovice he'd described.

"My school," he said. "Come." He went right to the door, swung it open and went in without hesitation. We followed him into a large room. "Is this the very room?"

"Yes."

"Mrs. Zhupan, right?"

"Yes. Mama Zhupan we called her. My teacher."

I had heard the name many times. Another of his female protectors, she shielded him from the bullies who threw stones at the only Jew in the class, in the several classes combined in the one room. She had understood, at last, when he balked at a ham sandwich offered at school lunch and found him something he could eat.

He gazed around for a moment and then strode up to the blackboard, picked up a piece of chalk and wrote something in Cyrillic letters on the board.

"Eva" he said, "this was the very first thing she wrote on the board when we came to school."

Eva shook her head, ruefully, sympathetically.

"What does it say," I asked.

"Christ is risen."

The caretaker arrived, a stout shy woman, whom my father nearly cajoled into helping him recover one of the folk songs they used to sing at school. He hummed something, encouraging her to join him. He had her giggling before we left.

After a few more bumpy minutes in the car, my dad leaned forward, staring intently through the windshield, and finally pointed: "There, there it is." We had entered a small valley, with a house just discernible behind trees, a concrete pen to the side. Dad had always spoken of the rolling foothills of the Carpathians, and there they were, low hills in the distance, and a spread of gleam that had to be the river, the Latorice. We got out and walked. A rooster crowed, and we could hear the bleat and bleat-back of lambs and the snuffle and grunt of pigs in the pen.

A figure approached us from an adjoining field, with the swing and high step of wading through grass, and began calling. My father, smiling and waving, awaited the welcome on a level piece of ground beside cherry trees. The small, middle-aged woman delivering it had the faintest hint of Asia in her cheekbones and eyes. She wore layers of clothes despite the heat, an apron over a dress over pants. For some reason it was her lone figure coming toward us that brought the isolation of the spot to me, how deep in the country, how thin the marks of human habitation, how different his childhood from mine. He had spoken often of the long winters, the battle to keep warm and fed. Despite the green abundance of this late spring, nearby trees heavy with cherries, I had no trouble envisioning the struggle as I swept the camcorder over the landscape before lowering it for an introduction and intermittent translation—from my father, and Eva as

*At my father's elementary school in Kustanovice. On the blackboard he has written, in the center, his teacher's name, Mama Zhupan, as they called her. Above and below are the first words she had chalked on the first day of school—"Christ is risen."*

*Dad picking cherries, yards away from the site of his birth, eating as he did when he was a boy*

well, though her Ruthenian, the native language of this region, was better than her English.

This was Yulia, daughter of Ilona, a childhood neighbor and friend of my father's, another protector. They launched into an animated conversation in Ukrainian, though a solemn note arose immediately. My father had asked after Ilona; sadly, she had died soon after his last visit. More exchanges of inquiry and news followed; a conversation, a country conversation, like those I'd heard in Ireland among those who had met after a long time—a list of names, who was related to whom, age at death. I needed a very few words to get the gist. Ordinary deaths in ordinary circumstances.

In a matter of minutes, others joined us: Yulia's daughter and son and a little granddaughter, fair-haired and shyly curious. My father went right to the little girl, his rapport with children instant. These encounters, so familiar, were always a bit disturbing for me; his magnetism in those moments of connection with a stranger's child was very different from the long run with his own.

I hadn't wanted to interrupt but did. "Dad, the hut: where is it?"

"Didn't I say? It fell to pieces. Years ago."

He told me that where we were standing, this flat area, was where the hut had been, the place he had been born.

"And do you see this ground right here, how it goes down? I was babysitting for Shmuel and we had a cradle that, if you didn't prop it up, it would roll over and he was swaddled and all that stuff. Well, I don't know, I went off to play and Jason…I mean, Shmielcoo…" He paused and shook his head. Not the first time he had confused my name with his brother's. "He rolled out and you see this heavy, heavy tall grass? We couldn't find him for hours."

For a change he had to translate for others what he had said to me. He looked for a few seconds first down the slope of the meadow and then all around. I stood behind him trying to see what he saw, tracking through the lens of the camera.

Conversation flowed around us, Volodya and Eva participating fully. Volodya and I took turns with the camera. We had drifted over to the cherry trees, following my dad, who was intent on pulling down the branches to get at the fruit. Soon everyone was grazing.

"You see now, Jason, how we used to have our lunch."

"I see how short guys didn't eat as well as tall guys."

Behind us, across the way, seeming to emerge from a thicket, an old man made his way toward us, slowly, accompanied by what I took to be a son, around my age, neatly dressed in contrast to his ancient-seeming father. The elder was ragged in clothing as well as in body, missing most of two fingers and the thumb on his left hand and many teeth. Horschak was their surname, and in the midst of his son's greeting, the old fellow closed on my father, who assumed an extra gentle manner prepared, apparently, for a dodderer. I trained the camera on them as the man launched into something about Kabastura, a name I recognized as the local landowner from whom my grandparents had rented the vanished hut. Then another name followed in a flurry of sentences. "Yitta Feiga," I heard him say, with particular emphasis, and to my father's joy. He knew my grandmother.

My father said, smiling, "He says there was no other such a seamstress anywhere." He asked Mr. Horschak a question, clearly a leading one. The reply had him laughing.

"Maybe not in all the world, because he doesn't know the world, but in Carpatho-Ruthenia."

*Dad reminiscing with Mr. Horschak, a schoolmate who knew his family*

Dad in delight put his arm around Mr. Horschak for a moment, then evidently tried to test him.

"Zhupan," Mr. Horschak said.

Again my dad smiled broadly at the response. The old man was a little troubled, according to Dad, that he couldn't immediately remember his old teacher's native village, which wasn't Kustanovice. He talked himself through it aloud, though, and came up with the answer.

Then Horschak came back with a test of his own, pointing to himself. It seemed to be a guess-my-age test. Dad took a few tries, generously low, I gathered. He was eighty-three, and though he was four years older than my father, Dad thought they had been in the same schoolroom.

As Mr. Horschak continued his recollections, my dad said, "He says he'd see the nets, from my father. My father was a fisherman."

Dad asked him about the brothers who had lived here, starting with Hersch..., but could not finish even that first name before Mr. Horschak reeled off the three names.

"He wants to know how many children Herschko has." Dad answered, and then tried to ask about himself, about Meilech. And again he was interrupted, a mock rebuff and a gesture with the maimed hand. Dad laughed: "He says he knows who I am."

Then Mr. Horschak asked about Shmiel. And my father told him that he was dead. "Boh," Mr. Horschak said in a long sigh, an exhalation of something like disbelief, a no, not so.

But how could he have been surprised?

My father gave a brief account. I recognized some words by now in several languages: train, bridge…and Auschwitz in any language.

They reminisced some more, remembering half a dozen other people, the two, perhaps three Jewish families in the village. They wrestled together with memory, prompting each other by turns, and filling in—each coming up with names, or parts of names, then the other confirming or completing, both joyful at the retrieval from so far back, joy merely at the recovery of those Jewish family names and the pure exercise of memory, not for a moment considering what had happened next, what must have happened to them, terrible things to every one of those people, varying only in degree.

They took a breath, and my father smiled and nodded, then sang out, "Vol—od—ya." He was ready to go.

But there was something more Mr. Horschak had to say. "He is very happy we have come," my dad said, and then he listened, concentrated, translated. What arrived in English already had the melody of what it was in Ukrainian: "He says there was and there will never be again. There were rivers, there were people and they are no longer. There in the earth that's where the truth is. While he lives he wants to see the world, there's plenty of time to lie underneath the ground."

We went slowly toward the car, saying our good-byes to everyone beside the well where his mother had drawn water, an octagon of cement brown with age at the base and lidded with a rusty iron plate. We looked through a square opening at the top, my father and I, but couldn't even make out our outlines down in the black water. I took my own last look back toward the river and saw in the nearest field a man heaping a hayrick. Maybe he was Yulia's husband. He must have been there for some time, busy with the work of the present.

# 7

*My father, who has come through much to get here*
*prepares to turn the page.*

. . . . . . . . . . . . . . . . . . . . . . . . . . . . . . . .

*There are so many losses and Meyer is little to him,*
*so few survivals and a picture something but not enough.*
*The dearest faces to him from then*
*are faces not in this book,*
*faces of which there are no extant images*
*outside of memory.*

AS WE LEFT KUSTANOVICE, my dad stared out the window, reflective. At one point he said softly, "We went down this road in a carriage. It was all mud then."

"A carriage? To shul?"

"Never by carriage to shul, Jason, for sure. We would walk, miles. And anyway, it was back the other way, near Bukovina. No, I meant when we left the village for good. We went in a…wagon, with everything piled up. A skinny old horse pulled and the rest of us had to help, pushing uphill and holding it back to go down."

"You left because…?"

"The peasants stopped bringing my mother work. And the anti-Semitism was more and more—which was why they stopped. The farm labor stopped, too; they wouldn't hire her. And my father wasn't doing the fishing."

So the family moved to Munkacs, where a vibrant—if fractious—Jewish community constituted almost half the population of a city of about twenty thousand. The beauty of forest and field and hills hardly compensated for privation and threat.

And now we returned in real time, going back the way we had come, though I barely heard the conference about directions. I was thinking of Horschak and his surprise at hearing of Shmuel's death. It was hard to square with the anti-Jewish feeling in the village, children throwing rocks at my dad, the relentless anti-Semitism. Horschak seemed well disposed, really quite sweet and natural, greeting his old Jewish neighbor and schoolmate. Had sixty or seventy years of history made the difference?

Well, the relations between ethnic groups in this area were as complicated as that history. Ruthenians, Ukrainians, Russians, Czechs, Jews— governed at one point or another after WWI by Hungary, Czechoslovakia, the Soviet Union. Not to mention Nazi Germany. It was absurd to even attempt to detect the sway of competing nationalisms in the interaction, but still I had to wonder. The old man knew the Jewish families, their names from the villages around. The point was, Horschak didn't seem the sort to have harbored ill feelings toward the Jews, whatever their politics. Though hating Jews isn't particularly about politics. All sorts participated, looting or standing by approvingly. And there was plenty of testimony about that in Munkacs, about those who swarmed into abandoned Jewish homes as well as those who simply observed the dispossessions and dislocations. That photograph I had seen of that group of Jews with their few remaining possessions in bundles, driven to the brickworks—who had taken the picture? And why?

The politics of my father's family had been survival. Jews of this region were generally known to have been pro-Hungarian at first and grateful, earlier, for equitable treatment under the Czechs. The fact that my dad had been at a Ukrainian-speaking school together with his neighbors suggested a degree of common allegiance, despite the relative separateness the Jews maintained. So what had Horschak thought of the cataclysm that ended this coexistence, the mounting pressures that culminated in deportation and what followed? How could he have been surprised at Shmuel's death? No, it must have been feigned, a kind of politeness, sympathetic maybe, and a way to avoid a discussion too complicated for the meeting, beyond the social. What could he have said, the old man? *Those damn Germans, those Hungarians. We were sorry, some of us.*

Little to do then, perhaps. Little to say now. And my father cooperated with the boundaries of reminiscence, keeping mostly within the limits of Kustanovice in the twenties and early thirties, in his childhood.

When we reached Munkacs, we pulled over in front of a sizeable block of a house, a stucco exterior—in the tan-to-yellow range—masking its age. I asked my dad about it.

"This is where we lived when we moved to Munkacs," he said.

Not the house above, but the basement below. We walked around to the side, to a bright green wooden door. As we crunched the gravel down the path, the current owner emerged. Dad explained, and the fellow, affable enough, fetched the key to the basement and opened it for us.

This residence, despite the dark and damp, had been an improvement in family circumstances. The exchange was rural poverty for the urban sort, with hope of better. Relatives were going to help, and the move did provide work for my grandmother, laundering in other basements and in the river. My uncle Harry had been apprenticed to a tailor, and my dad too, after a couple of years in a Czech school as a mechanic. Shmuel, young as he was but early to maturity in size and strength, contributed by hauling wood—first with Dad and then on his own. Yet even imagining the place clean and freshly painted did not relieve the dimness; there were only a few small windows, high on the wall, and no fire would unchill the stone walls.

But good things had happened here. Harry, protecting their mother from an assault from her husband, who had threatened her with his cane, knocked my grandfather's tooth out. This story was always told emphasizing how out of character the violence was for Harry, but I had seen him flailing a belt at his kids. Harry ran from the house, but my grandfather, aware then that his violence could be opposed, soon left the family forever. That was a very good thing, and in its wake better days did come.

My father, who had been speaking to the owner, turned to me, sweeping his hand around the room. "You see this. We moved all the furniture to the walls and danced in here sometimes. I had lessons in the workingman's club, but here we danced. We sang. My uncle Joseph would visit a lot, on Shabbos. He was shy. He sat on the side and listened when we had company. My mother sang. And Shmuel, Shmuel had a beautiful voice—he would sing for us, solo."

He translated for Volodya and Eva.

It was hard to imagine the brothers and my grandmother singing down here and practicing ballroom dance. I thought of my parents dancing. They never seemed more in harmony than when they were—at bar mitzvahs or weddings. As I looked around the room, it occurred to me that the constrained space here had helped develop the control my father exhibited on an unconstrained dance floor. So much of his joy seemed to come from such contrast that he must always have been conscious of being released from confinement of one sort or another.

A familiar sense of a confinement of my own nagged at me, and I became impatient to leave. It wasn't just the airlessness of the basement. All of what I was seeing made emphatic how hard Dad's life had been, even before his Holocaust odyssey. I had wanted to see all these places, the sites of the stories, but I wanted to expand our view now. Shmuel was on my mind. He had lived here too, and had been mentioned from time to time throughout the day, but he seemed very much in the background still, part of the general scene. And I felt acutely right then my desire to bring him forward into the center of things. I knew we were headed for the Yiddishe Gasse, the Jewish neighborhood where the ghetto had been established. That would be easy to find, but we weren't yet sure of the location of the brickworks, where Shmuel and so many others were loaded onto the train to Auschwitz.

As we left, I asked about the animals. That had been another comfort, a joy really, for Dad and Shmuel especially—a dog that obeyed commands in three languages and Miriam, the cat that fetched.

"Didn't you tell me Shmuel kept pigeons? Where was the dovecote?"

My father smiled at the memory. "Yes, yes—just back there behind the house. All the sounds."

"Like rumbling stomachs, right?"

"Ha, ha, no; the cooing like babies. Shmuel loved them. Oh, he would open the door and out they would fly up into the sky, and always they came back."

We drove to the city center to get some food, parking near the pedestrian area in view of the striking mint-green city hall. There were some errands to run. Eva had to drop some things off, and we had to be provisioned for the next couple days on the road. I left the group to stretch my legs, to have a look around. I took my camera, but I wasn't sightseeing. Though I hardly admitted it to myself, I was looking for the background of a sixty-five-year-old photo, the Vishniac picture of Meyer Tsits and the "wealthy citizen."

Dad had said it was taken somewhere on the Corso, the old promenade, except I could find no such name on any map. Perhaps he wasn't right about the location. I certainly couldn't go by the street signs; the names had changed, more than once. A small group of Zionists had convinced the Czech authorities to allow Yiddishe Gasse to be renamed for Judah Ha-Levi, poet-philosopher-physician of medieval Toledo, and the forbidding Hasid Shapira had it redone again as "The Way of Repentance." That wasn't far from here; Corso too should have been near city hall, I was sure of that.

But who should I ask? Not my father, surely. What would I tell him—that I was looking for the location of an old photograph precisely because of some doubt about him, about his utter innocence? And that wouldn't even be quite true—because in my half-thought, my fantasy, I didn't actually expect to seek and find, but that I would somehow *happen upon* where Meyer had walked that day, that photographed moment. And that discovery would be a sign, auguring success. Because if, by a sort of grace, things only half-sought would reveal themselves, why then, what we searched for in earnest might also come to us.

*In the basement that was Dad's first home when the family moved to Munkacs*

Besides, it shouldn't have mattered whether I found the exact spot. If it was important to me to commune in some way with the mentally challenged man by locale, wasn't I doing it sufficiently? He would have walked so many places on these streets, whatever their current names.

He would have been right here, in front of this theater, across from city hall. If not in his ordinary rambles, then perhaps when they marched the Munkacs Jews down this way—Lilly had spoken of it and I'd seen a picture—the arched windows of the Star Hotel in the background. But perhaps they trucked Meyer, as they did with the disabled; his shuffling walk might have gotten him beaten or killed on the way, had he been marched. Nothing here memorialized the events. No sign, no historical marker commemorated how the Jews had been driven to the brickworks, beaten by the gendarmes. A few Germans had been in active attendance, but the Hungarians needed no instruction. They had driven the Jews into the ghetto near here, doing some killing along the way. That took place in April 1944, on the last day of Passover. Many well-off Jews had been abducted by various locals and tortured to extract information about suspected hidden valuables. Then, on May 15, the gendarmes drove the city's Jews to the brickworks, almost emptied by then of the countryside Jews who had preceded those of Munkacs—to the brickworks, to Auschwitz, to the chimneys. I knew from Lilly that she and Shmuel had been brought down this street in front of the Star Hotel, across from the theater, both buildings here unchanged.

I wandered, mostly in the pedestrian reserve, looking above the contemporary storefronts for a sense of the original appearance of buildings. The city center had been well preserved, relatively undamaged from the war as liberation came late and without great resistance by the Axis. By then, the Hungarians had tried to abandon the Germans. Only the war against the Jews would be pursued to the last moment. Eichmann had walked these streets while he was here in this city to arrange the final solution for the region.

I continued walking, dimly aware of the charm of the city center but mainly directing my gaze upward, ready to be persuaded at the slightest clue in the second stories and rooflines that what I was seeing could be what I had seen before in pictures. I was sure I was in the old places—whatever their names—moving along streets that Meyer Tsits drifted around, chased his tormentors through, even if I hadn't found the precise spot of the photograph. I had brought that picture to my dad nearly twenty years earlier, and if I could have brought him to the actual street and said, "Right here, Meyer, hands in sleeves, shuffled beside the man in the *shtriemel* to Shabbos dinner," that would have been something of my own somehow. I took some video of the square, the landmark buildings, but it was time for me to return to the meeting place, the parking area at the border of the square. I could make out my three traveling companions standing by the Lada. No surprise that my father should be early. He was beckoning.

"Hey, Jase, come. Sheebeets. Let's go." He turned to walk with me still yards off, and I had to catch up. What was the rush? Was he in a hurry to begin now, to tend to Shmuel, to start the final portion? A block or two away was Yiddishe Gasse, the Jewish street. The adjoining streets, with their concentration of Jewish households, had made for easy enclosure, and two ghettos had been formed here, with Yiddishe Gasse the dividing line. In moments we were standing in front of a large beige stucco building, a former synagogue the maps said, affixed with a molded plaque with a legend in Cyrillic and Hebrew beside a map of Israel flowing into a large menorah, branching over the top, whose central stem became a chimney issuing strands of smoke.

My father began to translate, but the Hebrew was fairly easy for me to decipher. "In the year 1944 from this place were taken thousands of Jews to their deaths." We were at the ghetto, and this large old, shabby building had been a synagogue. In and around here they were gathered, penned, starved, and terrorized, prepared for deportation. Harry had already been taken to forced labor a few years before—as had so many adult men, a practice ended by the German takeover. But Shmuel had been here, as had Lilly, my great-aunt Irene, and about sixty others of the family—more than sixty souls, my father would sometimes say.

But not now. Now he just led me down the street to the doorway of a store with a tile floor, a small stationer's shop, which had been the *mikveh*, he told me, the ritual bath where women would come after their periods and where converted Jews were required to bathe.

I nodded back toward Volodya and Eva. Understanding the gesture, my father translated. Both seemed a little subdued, Eva's steady, strong energy on low and Volodya's perfect tact evident in his silence. Were we all of us preparing for something to happen? Giving my dad some space? He had hurried us here, perhaps to get on with things, to reach something painful and get it over with. I had been filming his observations but also waiting, though I didn't know for what.

We went behind the building, into a small alley. He was talking now about pots, the communal cauldrons, which had been back here, and pointed at a place near a row of hoardings, metal and wood, with no buildings behind them. Had they been razed? Had they taken up the cobbles, too? Because everything underfoot was packed dirt and small stones.

Dad said, "They were full of boiling water, there to *kashe* the dishes you used during the week and make them Pesachdikke."

He was speaking of koshering for Passover, and it was the day after Passover that the ghetto had begun filling: two days to force the people in; about five weeks between ghetto and brickworks. Were that Passover and the aftermath on his mind, or had the site simply triggered a random memory? Of course, he hadn't seen the ghetto the Hungarians and Germans had made of this place any more than I had. He had known only the vitality and bustle of Jewish life in these streets, not its extinguishing. For a moment I felt us to be in a similar position. We had heard. We had our witnesses, our survivors. In fact the same ones, and strangely enough my questions to them fifty years later may sometimes have gotten more than what they volunteered to him so soon after. We had heard. We had read. But the specific experience we were attempting to approach was one to which we were both relative outsiders.

I confess now to those thoughts, but the thoughts that immediately followed were correctives and perhaps made me feel as small as I deserved— for his analogies to that experience were infinitely closer than mine. He had been in the railcars—not as crowded, bound not for Auschwitz but for slave labor—but he knew what it was to fear for his life among people who would just as soon take it as not, and he had certainly encountered those who wanted to take it. If he was recoiling, or delaying, at imagining this ghetto, it was likely because it wouldn't much stretch his powers of imagination. Nor would he have to imagine the faces. He knew them. They were dear faces.

I knew Lilly hadn't told him about being on the same transport with

Shmuel until her stunning revelation at Thanksgiving dinner. She wouldn't have considered, perhaps, that she had anything of substance to add to the story. But had Lilly been so absolute in her refusal to speak that she hadn't mentioned my father's aunt Irene? His mother's sister had been in this ghetto among the many thousands crammed into its confines, and she was alone, with no one willing to take her in. She was widely known to be a communist, and people were terrified that she would bring even more misfortune on anyone sheltering along with her. Irene had asked to stay with Lilly's family. Despite the connection with Irene's nephew, my uncle Harry, already Lilly's serious boyfriend, Lilly's mother had refused. Lilly, though, had sneaked her into their home so she could sleep with others in the apartment's kitchen. Irene returned the kindness in Auschwitz by getting extra rations to Lilly and her sisters. I wanted to ask Dad what he knew from Lilly about the ghetto, and from others and who they were. But at that moment he was ahead, still full of purpose, leading us farther down the street. He stopped at a sharp bend.

"Here had been an older house, which they tore down to build this one," he said. "We lived here."

I had forgotten the family had also lived on Yiddishe Gasse, the brothers and my grandmother, two rooms above ground. My grandmother had a room of her own, in a former kitchen with a defunct oven. The boys were bringing home some money then and my grandmother would not have had to work so hard, but it was already too late. Soon she couldn't work at all. She had started coughing, and the coughing continued and worsened and there was blood. What had begun in that dank basement, in perpetual twilight, ended in December 1941. My grandmother, Yitta Feiga, was forty-three years old when she died.

Here had begun a grief that would be with my dad always and that would surface from time to time. Its depth was a measure of his love for her and her gifts to him. But he was not revisiting that grief just now. He reviewed the personal events in Yiddishe Gasse for me in such a matter-of-fact way that our standing here felt like a sort of duty call, even more than posing before her gravestone, and done as much for me as for him, a place to take a son. No private communion followed, as at the cemetery. There were other things he might like to see, that he had spoken of, but they too were changed or gone. Eva had informed him. The ground might be there, as with his birthplace, but in the city, fields are soon filled, and structure succeeds structure. There had been a tennis club where he worked summers as a ball boy and saw how rich people conducted themselves. He learned tennis by watching. And somewhere under some building lay the soccer field that he and Shmuel were forbidden to visit by his father. They dared to go anyway, which cost them a beating.

These places no longer exist in those forms. A few months after his mother's death, he left Munkacs for Budapest and returned only once before the deportations. A bike mechanic living on his own in the big city, he returned in a new suit, indulging in the extravagance of a carriage ride from the station down Yiddishe Gasse. The first picture we have of him, the only one that survived the war, was from that trip. As he turned away from the house and toward me, there was something in his stance that made me think he might have come to the end of his story in Munkacs, that we would go on to different stories, to his brother Shmuel and the others. I wasn't surprised when he mentioned the brickyard then, with an air of finality: "Yeah, the *teglayar*. We must go to find out about it—I don't want to forget."

By "finding out," he meant he was unsure of the location but knew how to get directions. We would head for the synagogue. We made our way back up the street—now named for the rescuer of Jews, Wallenberg—and approached an enclosure, walled off by metal panels. Only a few hundred Jews were left in the town, and a handful were here, behind what I believed had been the Munkacser Rebbe's shul, though other Orthodox would have attended along with the Hasidim. Unlike the synagogue with the plaque up the street, this one was still functional, though not in great shape: the cracks in the stucco and general shabbiness were discernible from a considerable distance.

As we entered the yard, my father greeted four or five old men with handshakes and *sholom aleichem*. The Hebrew told the men we were Jewish, and an exchange of other identifiers followed—a precis of life stories in several languages, traded with my father. One fellow had to admit, to general laughter, that while nearly all of them had been trying to get out of Munkacs after the war for many good reasons, the Soviets not the least of them, he had come from Budapest and married a local woman and stayed.

I was able to follow some of the conversation, and as usual my father translated intermittently. I quickly dodged behind the camera, trusting that we would eventually get to our errand and with some idea of preserving narratives of survivor experience. One vigorous gray-haired gentleman in a Regina Tours ball cap, shorter than my father, had been in the labor battalions like my dad and ended up in a Soviet gulag. He smoked as they talked, going back and forth between Russian and Hungarian without warning. It turned out my dad had known his brother. After more trading of names and fates—of those in the yard and others, those who had returned to the city to leave again, and those who hadn't returned—Dad asked about the way to the brickyard. One of the men, who had said little else, indicated that he had walked the four or five kilometers himself in 1944. We would go by car.

Five minutes later we had parked. Volodya and Eva, chatting, led the way; I walked behind with Dad, videotaping. Not that there had been anything in particular of interest to record at that moment, but I wanted to remind myself that that's what I ought to be doing. There was plenty of activity on the wide, tarred street, but everything about the neighborhood declared it as at the margins—road signs that seemed to direct traffic elsewhere, spaces between structures. On our left were some smaller buildings and a long low one that appeared institutional, but no indication of what sort. Across the road was lots of scraggy greenery and, at last, the entryway to what was unmistakably a brickyard, lots of old sheds, chimneys, and—of course—bricks. A large overgrown field was full of them in stacks and rows. Clearly the yard had been restored to commerce for some time, though it appeared not to have been in very recent use.

The factory had been much expanded too from the original, according to what I had read. Only a few wooden buildings had stood here. Masses of people had been distributed over open ground, but in a fairly compact area, waiting for their turn to be crammed into the boxcars. Dad called me over to where he stood beside the rails, vegetation coming up through the rail bed, and the ties submerged in the ground. How could these not be the ones, the originals, from then—in the same ground, in the same earth? That at least should have been indisputable.

"In this direction, Jason, the rails, for memory's sake." He wanted me to film them. "These were the rails that were taking them from the brick factory to Auschwitz."

*Entering the great synagogue at Uzhhorod, now a theater with all Jewish symbols removed*

Them. People I knew, people I would never know, except through story, and people unremembered, unmemorialized, beyond recall in every way. Mothers and fathers, grandparents, and the children, a special horror in that. Thousands of the anonymous had been gathered here, but among them had been Shmuel, Lilly, and her brothers—also the sisters whom I sat with around the table in Brooklyn as a child—Miriam, Regina, Helen. All my father's people were brought here, taken from here: Aunt Irene, shy Uncle Joseph, and the stern tailor Solomon. The more than sixty souls.

I moved my focus down the spur of rust-pitted rails that still must join more rails, rails to rails to rails all the way to Poland. I was filming the chimneys and thinking of the other chimneys when a caretaker rushed toward us, flailing his arms and shouting. We were trespassers. Before anyone who could actually communicate with him, could speak or explain, I shouted back. In a tone that matched his, modulated slightly, perhaps a little louder, I spoke as I moved toward him, fairly sure that he wouldn't understand most of my words but not much concerned about it.

"Jews here," I said, briskly, aggressively chipper, "Yivrai, Zhid—coming to see where our family was taken from, asshole. And by the way, where's a sign, a plaque, something to show that they went, that thousands went, all the Jews of Munkacs, and miles around? Go call the fucking cops."

Bewildered, the man shut up, but stood his ground. Volodya called out something that even in his strong tones sounded conciliatory. My father put his hand on my forearm and we turned to leave the yard. We left Munkacs too.

That encounter marked the emotional end of that long, important day, though we did make a couple of additional stops in Uzhhorod, forty kilometers from Munkacs, where we would overnight ahead of the journey's next step: the drive into Slovakia, in the direction of Auschwitz, and the search for the bridge. Those stops—a folk museum in the shadow of a medieval castle and the Uzhhorod synagogue, now a concert hall—added some color to my father's story and the story of the region's Jews. A low, whitewashed hut with a thatched roof at the museum approximated his first home, and the synagogue building was a magnificent Moorish revival building.

In the former synagogue, I left my dad with Eva and Volodya. He was talking to strangers, telling his own story in brief, and I recognized the Russian for "train" and "bridge." I tried to dismiss my familiar resentment, mild but distinct, that these stories were so readily told to strangers. His mission. His compulsion. But perhaps necessary. As I wandered, dealing with this rise of resentment, thinking about the events of the day, I gradually became aware that, in the impressive architecture surrounding me, there was not a single Jewish sign or symbol. It had been a famous synagogue. Its history had been cleansed. The Ukrainians had finished the job started by the Germans and Hungarians and whoever else. A complete excising. Not a trace.

# 8

*If they suffer memory for me,*
*maybe I can give them something in return,*
*the date they need to commemorate*
*the true anniversary of Shmuel's death*
*with yahrzeit candles—my bookishness of use*
*to them with S.S. diaries, maps of train routes.*

AFTER DINNER AT OUR UZHHOROD HOTEL, we all adjourned to the room my dad and I would share. The three Russian speakers distributed themselves on ends of the saggy twin beds and traded stories and jokes for a good couple of hours, till past ten—late for my father, who typically began wrestling with sleep earlier. Late for me, too—I found myself flagging after the full day. In what was becoming a pattern for the trip, I was left to my English-only devices, following some cumbersome efforts to understand the exchanges. I assumed invisibility by picking up the camcorder, a tactic I'd used several times before, partly to relieve their obligation to include me, transforming myself from potential participant to observer. I didn't record much, though, as the gathering seemed off-duty and, if the repetition of "Viagra" was any indication, off-color as well.

Eventually the others left and I began considering our early start the next morning and the search for the bridge. Thanks to Volodya, we knew the route the transport train had likely taken—through eastern Slovakia before angling north to the Polish border, and another seventy-five miles or so from there to Auschwitz. Somewhere along that route was the setting of Shmuel's escape. And death. Would that be around Presov? Or farther north? Somehow I had become fixed on Slovakia, a kind of momentum that proceeded from my initial uncertainty about the route, and then my attempt to mark all the river crossings on my maps. The details of the template-story had receded as the maps of Slovakia occupied me, and Poland—Poland itself, as a whole—got embedded in my mind as a destination, as if getting over the border were the goal. Of course, the end point wasn't the Polish borderland but Oswiecim, the town where the camp was situated, a distance into the country, and as I would soon discover, the bridge might well be within that seventy-five-mile stretch beyond the border.

As we were turning in—I was already in bed, too sleepy even to read—my father mentioned the Dukla Pass, a notch in the Tatra Mountains right on the Slovakian-Polish border and site of a famous battle in September 1944.

"Where the big tank battle was," I said, "right? Russians and Germans?"

"Maybe we would see something of the monuments. So many Russians died there, and Germans."

I was surprised. My dad had been rescued by Red Army troops near the end of the war and later recruited into an intelligence unit, working as a translator, but when he spoke of this time he usually focused on their brutality. "This is a place you want to visit?" I asked.

"I knew some soldiers who had been there."

"Your unit? Like Smirnov or Dinsky?"

"No, not them, but others we were with. And that battle.... If the Russians hadn't gotten through and come when they did to my area, who knows what would have happened to me. I was running out of time. You know the *mamzer* foreman of the farm was suspicious already I was a Jew."

In August 1944, on the run from the labor camp he had escaped, my dad had disguised his identity and found work as a farmhand at an agricultural school on the outskirts of Budapest. Some poor Jewish soul, being carted somewhere on a truck, had seen my dad in the fields and called out his real name.

"Well, sure. I understand that, the Russians were your liberators."

"And Volodya—you know he lost his uncle there, was killed in the battle."

*Close to the Ukrainian border in Slovakia, my father in front of a Soviet tank memorializing the liberation of Slovakia*

So the memorial trip acquired another memorial dimension, for another uncle. Our ferryman had his dead too. But who wouldn't in this part of the world? Millions of casualties, soldiers and civilians. Besides, as I understood by then, Volodya was more than a ferryman, more than our Charon taking us over rivers for a glimpse of that other country. By now it was clear that my father considered him a friend—enough of one to allow distraction from the main focus of our trip. (Though I already had ample evidence that my father needed to lose focus from time to time, even—or maybe especially—in the midst of these locations so significant to him.)

Volodya had taken my dad around Munkacs before. He knew his story, had driven both my parents, probably in this same car, around some of the settings. I understood too that in this part of the world, gentile friends were protectors to my father. Nearly every time he mentioned any of his childhood companions among the peasants, it was as protector. He had needed them. Volodya had been reliable in the past, had proved himself. Though he hadn't seen my father in years or remained in contact, he retained the status of an intimate acquaintance. He was friendly to Jews, too—he was Eva's friend, for one thing, and he had dated a Jewish girl—so he was never just a driver. He would have to be something more. Without question we were obliged to include the Dukla battlefield in our itinerary.

But what would this detour do to our search for the bridge? Though I made no objection, I hadn't checked the map. Not that it was a huge change to the route; the distances were relatively small, and the early start would give us plenty of time for wandering. Yet as minor a deviation as it was, the route to Dukla was east of the railway and where I believed we should enter Poland.

"But you will remind him we want to go some of the way Shmuel went—the bridges, yes, but the route too."

"Yes, I have told him. We will do the best we can."

Had he told him? The best we can? Exactly the phrase Volodya had used in Munkacs in Dad's translation. Had they discussed my questions, my insistent questions about the route, and decided together to alter the route? Given what, the inaccessibility of the tracks? And failed to tell me because it wasn't exactly as I wanted or thought we had agreed? I was off and running—from that phrase, from the detour—deducing that they had discussed the matter without me. And, as so often in my relationship with my dad, I felt not only at cross-purposes but excluded in some essential way, as if my own perspective was always secondary.

But so what? Never mind. They discussed plenty without me; they talked all the time, surely about the route, too. I calmed myself; I would be in the car with the map. At least I would be alert to what was going on and could say something. I would make myself understood if I had to. But it wasn't only the limpness of the bed that troubled my sleep.

Breakfast looked like it could have been by special arrangement for us, with none of the other guests down yet. Eva was on her way back to Budapest and we bade her a brief farewell—we'd all be meeting there in a couple of days.

The Slovakian border was ten minutes down the road, and the guards were as sleepy as we were. Passports stamped, we left the Ukraine, driving into the brightening day. The weather had cooperated all along, steady sunshine and comfortable temperatures. Dad and Volodya chatted and I took in the rolling countryside, hilly and pretty, the road curving along what seemed the most level parts, taking advantage of the topography. I took some footage of the landscape.

I don't quite understand how my father's dedication speech happened. Not far into Slovakia, we stopped at a war memorial, a tank on a plinth, which I started filming. I was not entirely at ease with the video camera. There were scenes I wanted to preserve—landscapes, people we met along the way. But I found myself using it often as I would a still camera. And I was caught by the impulse, most often followed, to record things in a notebook, and wouldn't necessarily get out the camcorder.

But on this occasion, I did. Did my father indicate he had something to say? He wouldn't have just walked into the frame as I taped, though he might have started talking when I trained the camera on him. He must have sensed, though, as I did, that we were now launched properly on the quest. So, in front of the tank, with us newly crossed into Slovakia and the camera rolling, he spoke:

"OK, we are in Slovakia on our way on our search to find the river, the place where my brother jumped in and was eventually killed. We can consider it, my son and I, a kind of memorial, even if we don't find it, at least to be in the area where it happened to show respect for those that perished. We hope that we are going to find the precise place but it will be very difficult."

There it was: a kind of invocation, a preface…and a hedged bet. We would make an effort and the effort alone needed to be sufficient because the outcome would be uncertain. I hadn't examined my own attitude toward our chances. I'm not naturally optimistic, but I believe I was so focused on the process that I hardly considered failure, though I suppose a good deal of my focus was the attempt to avoid it. My father was preparing us, fair enough. The idea of difficulty had been a little lost to me in my concentration on rivers and bridges, or rather the other way around—did it signify anything that he had mentioned the river but not the bridge?

The bet was legitimate, and I appreciated his effort to make even failure a sort of success. But now that he had mentioned it, no, not for me it wouldn't be. I thought success was possible, even probable. Especially if we examined every bridge after a certain point. Also, the idea of showing "respect for those that perished" struck me as a peculiar thing to say. We were looking to honor only one, weren't we? Was Shmuel to be considered representative? Even the word "perished" struck a false note, felt romanticized. He had adopted something of a public voice; he *orated*. But who was he addressing? And I *was* recording his words. My attempts at filmmaking were weak, yes, but they were, or would become, our home movies, meant for us. If what I captured was ceremony, then it was private, closed, family only.

Back in the car, my turn in front for legroom, I took out the big map and tried to locate us. I wanted to talk about the route since I thought Volodya had moved off the main road. But my eye fell on a name I recognized. Jelsava. Jolsva in Hungarian. A town in central Slovakia I knew from my dad's stories.

I swiveled in my seat and showed him the awkwardly creased map. "Dad. This would be Jolsva, right?"

"Yes."

"We'll pass near there, won't we? Ask Volodya."

He answered vaguely, his eyes on the hills. "There is nothing much there. Even then there wasn't."

My dad had been in two forced-labor camps in 1944: a transit camp in Jolsva in the spring, where he had dug a foundation for a bunker using pickax and shovel, and, from May on, an industrial plant in Budapest (expropriated from Jewish owners) called Csepel. In both places he was abused and beaten and exposed to bombing raids, and he had been reluctant to revisit them. On his trip to Budapest with my mother in 1991, they had posed for a picture at the Csepel gates, the gates through which he escaped, but he had not gone inside. That escape had begun in a sense at Jolsva, where he met a young man named Imre, his coconspirator and fellow escapee. I avoided mention of Imre right then, though—not to distract from what I was asking.

"Wasn't Jolsva where you got in trouble with that anti-Semitic soldier?" I asked him.

He turned toward me, focusing.

"Yes, was something like that—a man who wouldn't let me eat in peace, a soldier, and I hardly did anything...."

Suddenly he was talking to me almost as if we were alone. He had conversed so much with Volodya, exercising his Russian, but this seemed for me only, without the usual translation for Volodya.

"I didn't even know what I was doing, lifting a hand to half guard the soup, half push him away..."

But suddenly he stopped, dismissing the story with a wave of his hand. As in the past, he did not want to go into detail. So much had been told and retold, why not this? Was it as I thought, that he was ashamed somehow—that one of us had made such a hero-story out of it, or that it had ended so badly? Though not so badly as might have been. They had beaten him, a group of soldiers. And they whipped him too, I think, though that could have been another time. I wanted to know and wanted to know why these were among the stories that seemed to have faded out, even while there were so many occasions for speech about these incidents: for one thing, Lilly's sudden disclosures after years of refusal.

This reticence with the incident: could it have been one of those times when he recognized that others—like Lilly—had had it worse than he did? Not just the Jews in the camps, as he would hear later on the steps of the Erzsébet school in Budapest, but those with him, like Imre? Imre had had a terrible beating at Jolsva and was the hero of Jolsva for what he endured, overshadowing my father's experience. Was that part of the reluctance?

"What about that beating you got?" I persisted. "And other beatings there? You say so much about other things, other times and places. So little about this."

"No, no, I have said. Sure I have said."

"Not very much. I mean nothing like detail, and I heard less and less as I got older, anyway, about Jolsva."

I felt I could ask now, press a little, under the close conditions of the little car, the low ceiling, cocooned together, cave-feelings. I had certainly heard what sounded like a tone of confidence with Volodya when they were together in the front seat. Now I felt he was talking directly to me, still a telling but without any performance in it—that I could be for the moment a more valued receptacle than others, than strangers, for what he told. My memory of hearing about his life was of groups, tables, gatherings. He had had many audiences, and latterly formal ones, as he became an actual public speaker. The reason I wasn't an audience of one for him must have been more than him being put off by my resistance. Others were what he needed. Only the attention of strangers could seem adequate recompense for the outright cruelty of strangers past. If, with his story, he could win them over, especially gentiles, he might be safe. And his faith in humanity might be restored with their acceptance. Others like them, however faint the resemblance, made him feel he was nothing; these, whoever they were, could make him feel he mattered.

"Well, I wasn't there for so long, a couple months," he said.

"But it's not how long, right? But how the things that happened, how you feel, how, how..."

"Sharp?" he offered, relieving my search for a word but not my rising nervousness, which I couldn't have accounted for.

"Yes, sharp. I saw, in some tape of a presentation of yours, at a school, you referred to a Hungarian officer, a decorated war hero who was about to whip you. You looked into his eyes for a sign of some humanity, you said, and it wasn't there."

"That was Csepel," he said.

"Sure. But Jolsva was the first place they took you, the first experiences of what they were going to do. I think sometimes with the survivors who are willing to speak, what they don't talk about might be in some ways the most significant. At least with you; at least with what I want to know."

He stiffened. "What 'you want to know'? What is it you want to know?"

I hesitated a moment. "What affects you most deeply, I guess, which would say most about you as a person."

"Is that such a mystery?"

And here I balked, entirely. "Isn't everyone something of a mystery?"

What I wanted to say, needed to, but would not—was that it was mysterious to me how he could have had such anger in him and represented himself as—I don't know what—an apostle of love. In that same talk, at the school, with the missing humanity in the soldier's eyes, he had said that Holocausts can only be stopped with love. He didn't say where that love came from or how it ought to be applied, just as he didn't say much about the beating from the man with the uniform full of decorations, though he knew the specifics, the man's medals or ribbons.

But why would he want to relive the details without good reason? I had heard, in an archival recording, testimony from a man who had been in Jolsva about the same time as my father. He had spoken of an officer who randomly beat the forced laborers with a bull's penis. Apparently they are very durable and can be made into whips—not something the whipped would forget or necessarily be inclined to tell others about. The whippings my father referred to but did not describe were more formal, military punishments for infractions. But I knew from this other testimony of punishments he must have observed—strappado, for example, where a victim is hoisted onto tiptoes, a rope around his wrists with arms behind the back; also people being forced to balance in a squat, wrists and ankles trussed, with a broomstick behind the knees, hands between the legs and attached to the stick.

For a time, *the* story out of Jolsva had been what happened to his friend Imre Naiman, whom he met soon after arriving at the camp. The owner of the bicycle shop where Dad worked as a mechanic had arranged for him to be paired with a doctor to schlep the man's medical equipment in transit to Jolsva, which seemed insurance in the uncertain circumstances—though that equipment would never be used at the camp; physical labor was everyone's destiny, along with humiliation and violence. But being with the doctor also provided entree to an educated group, including the university student Imre. These men represented my father's aspirations. Not in religious terms, for they were entirely assimilated, but certainly in their attainments and cultivation. I'd always heard of Imre, a "devoted friend," in the most exalted terms. He was a romantic figure, handsome and heroic, for beauty and goodness were fully attached for my dad.

The heroism was first established by Imre's steadfastness in his love for Ilona, a Catholic girl. The relationship was uncontroversial for the two families but highly objectionable to a local priest, so much so that the man traveled twice from Budapest to the camp in Jolsva to demand that Imre sever ties with her. One night, Hungarian soldiers, guards at the camp, joined the effort, took Imre away, and beat him so badly his friends didn't recognize him. Yet Imre refused to give up the girl.

My father offered this incident always as an example of principled action, resistance, and heroism. But the story haunted me. It seemed to call for my own resistance to the idea that it was a simple story of heroism. It highlighted my own cynicism, for one thing. My dad offered me the story with all the judgment included, so why couldn't I simply accept it as an example of heroism? But wasn't the resistance particularly useless? He was going to be beaten anyway, so was it really heroic? Yet why couldn't I simply accept my father's version and leave it alone?

It was like those Bible stories that excluded psychology and left telling details for the audience to imagine. What did Abraham feel as he bound his son to the altar? What had Isaac been feeling, thinking, saying, particularly afterward, going down the mountain? My dad's versions of this story—"Imre and the Soldiers" or "Imre and Ilona"—were similarly light on crucial elements. Would Imre's denial of Ilona have meant anything? Wouldn't she have assumed there was duress involved? How would his rejection have been conveyed? Was he to write to her? But the mail was uncertain. No, of course, the priest would have carried the message. Surely Imre could have signaled to her within the writing. Surely she would have understood. Anyway, had Imre recanted love would the beating have stopped?

Surely all of the heroism was for nothing. The soldiers were Jew-beating—that's the point—miscegenation added some spice, but that wasn't the real motivation, was it? That's where I landed anyway. The soldiers were going to beat him, to practice the fine art of to-within-an-inch-of-his life. That had to be the nub of it. Ilona was an excuse. As dissatisfied as I had always been with my dad's interpretation, my own speculations made me feel worse, guilty about where my own interpretation had brought me, to an emphasis on the meaningless hatred.

If I pressed myself further, I could imagine that for Imre it was a thing they could not take, could not make him yield—a fidelity to self. A chance to preserve the self, in the refusal to deny his lover, an opportunity to believe one was dying for something. Just as my father too made this incident justify the high sentiments, the high words: the handsome young man, aristocratic, noble. For me the meaning—the possibilities for meaning—lay elsewhere, that's all.

I heard the name many times, Imre Naiman, with some description along with it. As with many of my father's stories, when these names came my way, I tried to see the people in my mind and to understand. But I couldn't make them—him—signify what my father had.

This story had a crucial follow-up. Before their escape from the labor camp, Imre, my dad's great friend and companion in that escape, held out the possibility of shelter at the house of a blind professor he knew. They could hide out till the Russians came. But when it came to it, there was no room for my dad, and he was left to face the streets with nothing but luck

*On the lookout for tracks, thinking constantly of Shmuel's transport, we were taken by surprise at this reminder that the trains still use them.*

to protect him. Hearing this story, as I did so many times, I thought of the university boy, the professor, and then my father, a dirt-poor country boy, a bicycle mechanic. Had he been easy to exclude on those grounds?

My father had trusted Imre completely. For him, what looked like fatal exclusion from the hiding place could have nothing to do with his friend. Months later, back in Budapest after his liberation, my father got a wonderful welcome from Imre and his mother, a reunion of great warmth, according to Dad. Soon again, though, he had to flee, this time from the Russians. He tried to locate Imre after the war but without success. Others had been found, but not Imre, and Imre hadn't found him. That must have meant something.

Dad and I had lapsed into an uncomfortable silence, which Volodya relieved by calling out and pointing. To our right we glimpsed a train paralleling the road between the trees and hills, our first indication that we were anywhere near the tracks, and our first of how difficult it might be to stay near. The four or five passenger cars, deep green except for a red car at the rear, all patched with graffiti, disappeared quickly. By the time we stopped and walked up a rise to get a proper view, there was only the stretch of tracks to see, until they too curved from sight.

I heard them talking behind me. The word I picked up on sounded like *most*—Russian for "bridge." By now I had the word in several languages. I felt certain there were rail bridges over rivers around here, wherever we were precisely, and whatever river was nearest—the Topl'a perhaps, as we had seen several towns in the region described as *nad Topl'ou*. Though we were still too close to Munkacs for any bridge we might find to be Shmuel's bridge, I stayed attentive. I recognized place names and pressed my dad for details. Where had such and such happened? Well then, about where? And now I was sure we were passing through territory he had zig-zagged around after liberation, when he had worked for the Red Army. As usual I had things to ask him about. Especially given the fact that we were headed for a battlefield.

I dozed off; a spot of drool marked the map I had on my lap. Out the window in the world, as well as on that map, I had lost the thread of the road. I looked over at Volodya and took a breath to ask him how long I had been out and where we were, and then surfaced enough to realize that I hadn't the words. He understood my disorientation and near-speech, and we exchanged a smile. Surprising to me, how thoroughly I had gotten accustomed to a very partial comprehension of what was going on, other languages, other landscapes. Even coming out of sleep. I would wait to have things clarified. I turned to check the backseat and saw that a nap was ending there as well. Partly the rousing had been accomplished by the road, which had grown narrower and more winding.

Volodya answered one of the questions I hadn't asked, glancing sidelong at the map a few times and, without actually touching the paper, making a shallow arc with his finger, somewhere between Košice and Presov. I gathered we had looped off the main highway. The road had very few cars on it, and Volodya drove with his typical pace and assurance. But why were we going this way?

Then I saw a raised area not far away. I couldn't see them yet, but I knew we were headed for tracks. We went through a little tunnel in the stone support and I caught the flash of water. A sign said Kysack; the river was the Hornad. We stopped in the middle of a road bridge from which, getting out and looking north over the Hornad, we could see the railroad bridge, a fairly short span over the river, with some railing we could hardly discern. The banks around it were steep and the bridge emerged from and disappeared into trees.

"Too soon, much too soon," I said aloud but not directed at anyone in particular. "We aren't halfway through Slovakia, much less half the whole way."

Volodya didn't seem to need a translation. He nodded, shook his head and shrugged, and waved his hand at the bridge. He spoke to my father, who told me that bridges on this stretch of road, and on to the north, were like this one: the rivers shallow, the bridges themselves of varying lengths. "Few kilometer," Volodya said—meaning it was only a short drive to a similar bridge across the Svinka. It would take no time, he added, but turned to look at both his passengers and said, "*Kak pozhelayete*"— as you wish.

I believe it was my wish he was referring to. At that moment, Volodya was more in tune with what I wanted than I was. My father may have reminded him, or he himself may have remembered, but before we'd set out, I'd expressed a desire not just to find the last bridge but to see something of what Shmuel saw on his way. I didn't want that one bridge to be everything, I suppose, and needed to communicate that. But in the long hours since, I had slipped back into an utter concentration on finding the final bridge, the last views he had. And now Volodya was reminding me of my earlier wish.

And what had Shmuel seen on that awful train ride, through the window, through the cracks and loose joins in the wood? Where had he been most of the time in the boxcar? Had he chanced to be among the last in and therefore near the window of his escape, or would he have had to work his way over, assert himself with his youth and strength? I pushed that thought away. He saw, could have seen, the dark, the flashes through the sides, in that long time of being together, holding Zlate Raisel, long silences, long thirst, long hunger, amid the stench, the groans, weeping, prayers, the clack of wheels on rails. Crossing a bridge would have changed the mechanical sounds. The human sounds would have continued even when train sounds stilled in those hours halted on sidings as troop transports passed.

We were north of Košice, but not that far. Nothing was that far in this country. Košice might have been the longest delay to this point, where the Germans took over from the Hungarians, a city with a major rail yard. Any delays had to be the places, mostly around the towns, with more than the single set of rails.

When had Shmuel begun to comprehend? A long argument had started somewhere. A long effort at persuasion, each to the other, Shmuel, Zlate Raisel—and they would leave off and begin again. Other voices would have surrounded them, speaking to them, perhaps—family, neighbors—those they had been with in the city, in the ghetto, in the brickyard. Shmuel was saying what he thought they—he and she, at least—should do, that there was something to do. And finally he would do it, by himself, off a bridge on that last morning, a morning like this one, an ordinary morning. Surely where we had stopped was far too soon, even for the talk. Hard to say. Impossible to know.

Volodya had indeed brought us much closer already to places Shmuel had likely been or passed through, and he would do more. We got back into the car and within a few minutes found another stone underpass. The only way to get a good view of this bridge was to clamber up the embankment beside the tunnel, which I did on my own. Volodya was doing as I asked, I now understood, in his quietly responsive way—a special resonance reserved for my father but some for me by extension. We were following Shmuel's path as I'd asked to do, at least some of the way, and these bridges made that obvious, vague as they were, for something more than finding a single spot: not just the doing but wanting to feel the doing of. To go some way with Shmuel, however faintly.

From where I stood in the scrub and weeds, perhaps a hundred yards off, it was hard to judge the span, but the bridge appeared to be merely a flat, darker extension of the track bed. The Svinka was a tributary of the Hornad and a good deal narrower. Did this bridge, and the previous, resemble the bridge we were looking for? My plan had been to see them all, every bridge, to make sure. Volodya had tuned in to that plan, but our stops did not represent his estimation of what was potentially *the* bridge—not at all. Yet looking at these structures was more than just reliving what Shmuel had seen—it also helped me work out how Shmuel's story, passed on to me in such a fragmentary way, mapped onto the real world we were passing through.

I'd obsessed about Slovakia and rail routes, attempting to locate the bridges in every internet archive I could find. Volodya hadn't indicated—beyond his basic, and accurate, map of the rails—whether he had been doing any calculations himself, expert as he was in rivers and the region generally. I'd reviewed the story in my mind over and over. I believed I had the details down. The survivors had told me, Harry and Lilly both—they had gotten it first, from Zlate Raisel herself in Munkacs. I had listened well enough, I thought, to make my calculations.

Then it hit me. Morning. Shmuel had jumped from the boxcar on a morning like this one. I had been *mis*calculating. I had been too fixated on geography. Zlate Raisel had said his jump was on the *last* morning of their journey, actually the final few hours before their arrival at Auschwitz. She had agonized over that. Perhaps he would have survived had he not, in those last hours…. I should have reckoned back from that, back from arrival at Auschwitz. He'd jumped on the last day, in the light—the transport had arrived on the twenty-first or twenty-second of May in the morning. It wasn't Slovakia at all. It couldn't have been. The train must have already entered Poland. Time was what I should have considered most, and in the simplest terms—not the rate of speed particularly, as there were too many long delays, the cruel side-shuntings—but the count of days as what was usually a twelve-hour trip stretched into something over seventy-two.

So, yes, I had been correct, it *was* too soon. But even sooner than I imagined. It would be later, in Poland, that the fateful bridge would appear—if it appeared at all. In the meantime, I would absorb the geography of Shmuel's journey, and defer to my father's wish to visit the Dukla Pass and its battle sites.

The countryside rolled, the road curved—the view of distant hills shifted to different windows. On and off we were among the folds of smaller hills. A road sign said Komarnik—hadn't I heard that name before? Dad's battlefields had been in Slovakia: Kom...something. I turned to him to ask. Something about his expression as he looked around, both sides of the car, an alertness, made me wonder what was going on with him. Was the terrain jogging his memory?

My father had been in some firefights, though these were among the undertold tales. One in particular I was set to ask about, the only time he actually admitted to shooting. When he first joined the Red Army he had been sent, untrained, directly to the front lines, a mistake they sorted out after a few days. He barely mentioned that interval. His reluctance about soldiering had been a disappointment to me as a child with some interest in guns and heroics, and as an older boy with the standard Jewish revenge fantasy. The deployment error corrected, he served as a translator with a special unit, which roved around, taking prisoners for interrogation.

The unit recruited him with a combination of presumed inducements—decent food and a handsome uniform—and threats. Its leaders assured him they could find him wherever he went; that was part of their job, after all. They were intelligence, NKVD. Smirnov, the captain, was a little scary. He'd played the promiser-threatener from the start and alternated between charm and frothing mania. My father would see plenty of both from him, as well as getting heavy doses of the prevailing attitude toward Jews among the comrades. But his good luck also brought him Dinsky, a Jewish sergeant, tough and tested enough to command respect with the troops and willing to mentor a fellow Jew. Dinsky had been in charge during the incident I wanted to explore.

"Dad, Komarnik…Komarno…. I'm thinking of the place where you were ambushed out in the country."

"Hey, this you remember, ha—that's really something." He was a little excited. "But ambush, I don't know. They were trying to surrender, I think, a pathetic bunch. Deserters maybe. We were out getting supplies from the farmers with Dinsky. It would be well west of here."

"They surrendered by firing on you? Well, yeah, I would remember. I have this image of bullets coming through leaves. And you firing back." The last point was what I had most in mind when I first heard about it, and now again.

He held his hand up, a just-a-moment gesture, then leaned over to Volodya and spoke in Russian. I heard "Dinsky" repeated several times, and a little ventriloquizing—Dinsky cursing in Russian. Volodya and my father laughed. There was more of the anecdote being translated than he and I had just reviewed.

"So, Dad, there you were, in battle…"

I wanted a replay of the thrill of my father fighting back. Maybe I also wanted to hear whether the account would be the same as always. He told the story: nothing I didn't recognize in the events or in my own responses.

He'd frozen, he supposed, when the shooting started. Ducking down by the wheel of the truck, he'd held hard onto his machine gun. And Dinsky had screamed to him, something like, "You son of a fucking whore, what are you fucking waiting for? Shoot, you Zhid piece of shit." A Jew himself,

116

Jewish slurs were nevertheless part of his cursing repertoire, and mothers always.

And my father had shot, the fear equilateral: of death from the enemy and of Dinsky's blazing rage. He swung out from the side of the truck and emptied the papasha—almost unconsciously, he said—finger on the trigger, spraying bullets in the direction the shots were coming from until the drum magazine was empty.

He paused to direct some Russian at Volodya, filling in some details, I assumed, and then continued. The shooting attracted Soviet reinforcements. In a matter of minutes, he said, the enemy surrendered. As angry as Dinsky had been, his praise for my roused-to-action father was as hearty. In the end, a mixed group of Hungarians and Germans emerged from their position. At this point in the story, my father turned to pathos: the soldiers looked worn out and hungry. One of the Hungarians was about his age, and my dad felt sorry for him. But they all came out alive, hands up, unwounded.

"All of them, really, every one of them?" I said in a flat tone. The words had come almost unwilled. I'm sure the men had come out. I didn't doubt the facts. The devil was in me, though, and my father sensed something was up and got wary. But this was hardly a time his son would get sarcastic, was it? Had I seen a flicker of his anger? No, that would have been for a younger me; now I'd get a sort of humoring.

"Yes, sure, every one, and we brought them in."

"But you, or somebody, went back to where they had shot from. Take a look around?"

"Why would we? No. We had supplies to bring, and now prisoners." A faint note of exasperation in his voice.

"Well, I was thinking the dead wouldn't have come out to surrender."

"Ach, Jason," he huffed.

"So, how could you be sure you didn't kill anyone?"

"They came out, they said that was all of them. This was a small group, cut off."

"OK, OK, Dad."

My next question would have been, why? Why was it so important that he did not kill any of those who tried to kill him?

Volodya looked back at him in the rearview mirror, but no more translation came. My father busied himself with something in the backseat, wrestling off his small jacket and poking around in the food. And I didn't say anything for a while. But I was thinking, along familiar lines, about the totality of my father's innocence, that master theme of his narratives, maintained even in the midst of battle. He had done no harm.

I would have wanted to kill those men, so I believed, not only because they had attacked but on the general principle of the cause they served, and the high likelihood of their attitude toward Jews. Yet the fantasy was less about what I would have done than it was my desire to have my father want to kill them. And I had an accompanying fantasy: that some observer was there who could say what happened with utter certainty, a witness or researcher with access to all the archives. It wouldn't be my father's story then, or only his, and I could leave it be, nothing to ask and nothing to be added.

He hadn't killed, he hadn't wanted to, and he hadn't even been fully conscious as he was firing. Never had I been hunted as he had, which I believed ought to have made him hate in return, and I hadn't been anywhere near combat, either. But I did recall the few times I'd been in fights, and the fewer times that my blows landed effectively and consistently. I couldn't really say I was thinking of anything. I'd later associate the incidents in some way with my father's self-forgetting rage. I was so deeply in the striking, the delivery of the fist, that there was no restraint I was aware of. If I had been shooting, seething in that heart-bursting fear, I imagine it would have been the same, perhaps not thinking clearly enough to think of "kill" but surely not withholding "kill" either.

Meanwhile, we came on an arresting tableau by the side of the road. Tanks sitting on large twin bases, head-on: a Soviet T34 positioned to crash over the top of a German Panzer 4. We had entered the killing ground, the valley of death, so called. This was Svidnik, beyond which was not "Komarnik" but Vysny Komarnik, and the border. Next, on a green hill close by, a Soviet fighter plane was perched above the road and, incongruously, at a little distance, a helicopter that was clearly not the right vintage. A precision job, if it had landed here. A tapering stone tower marked the entrance to the Czech and Soviet cemetery a few hundred feet on, behind which were statues and in front of them thousands of graves.

We stopped very briefly. We were on our way somewhere else, after all.

But we had been reminded; our narrowed view had widened. Millions had died, thousands in this valley, opposing the Germans—and Hungarians. This point in the journey that I had thought was "not yet Shmuel" was not only Shmuel, not only Jews. Volodya's uncle had died as a member of a Soviet army that had been cruel by so many accounts beside my father's— vengeful—but had made terrible sacrifices in fighting an indisputable evil. Maybe they hadn't died for Jews, but their deaths had been in the cause that redeemed the surviving remnant, my father among them. So, this was no detour, nor would we be "resuming" our route. These places were on our route, must be our route. Tacit Volodya, was this too exactly as you intended?

*Tacit Volodya*

# 9

*I have a plan to follow rivers*
*if only on the maps, until they intersect*
*the lines of track, and I will have the place*
*he died among those crossings.*
*How many trestle bridges can there be,*
*crossing as the rivers bend?*

THE BORDER CROSSING WAS REMARKABLY EASY, almost perfunctory, and the road through Dukla Pass was a good one, two lanes but quick and scenic—the irregular ranks of the Carpathian Mountains ahead of us, behind us the symmetrical ranks of the military graves. I thought about the cemetery we had seen, our last stop in Slovakia, and the monument where we paid our respects. If Volodya had been reminding us then that others had died, *his* others—his uncle killed in the army in which he too served, a generation later—the gesture had acquired another layer, mildly ironic. Russians weren't buried there. The graveyard seemed to have been reserved for the Czechs who fought alongside the Red Army at Dukla. So here still others appeared again, another set of others to supply further instruction in the historical complexities: Czechs and Slovaks—not Russian, not Ukrainian—and some Jews among each group, no doubt. I had remarked on none of that. Volodya and my father had been fittingly quiet.

Now we were in Poland. No one had to tell me we were nearing... what to call it? The zone of possibility? Of probability, as I'd have preferred to say? We were narrowing in, coming to that midway point between Munkacs and Auschwitz—in Poland, as I had realized overlooking the bridge on the Svinka. We had to be coming close to where Shmuel made his leap. No map needed yet, though I would soon be folding my map of Poland to display only its most southerly region. I could judge our direction from the position of the sun easily enough, but by now I could sense where we were headed, could tell when a curve in the road marked a real change. I was as attentive as a hooded kidnappee, or a deportee in a closed wagon—another of those thoughts I would have and then try to thrust off, unentitled to the comparison, to make an image out of that. We had been going north but turned west. I imagined I could feel the homing toward the tracks. We crossed a river, not very wide, and I made a mental note to check its thickness on the map; such a gauge might be helpful.

After a short discussion, apparently about regional music, my dad started singing, Volodya joining intermittently. A couple of Ukrainian folk songs sputtered up and guttered out, missing words, missing notes. Then "Vrt Sa Dievca," a Czech song my dad had often sung, from his childhood to mine. I remembered enough to get through the chorus with him, faking some of the words. Near-silence took over for a while: only the hum of the tires and the car's alternations of rhythms, sound, and sensation—rough stretches beneath, the sideways pull and push of the curves, the heat of full sun blinking on and off from different angles. A roadside shrine appeared, a large cross and a small box on a post. Above that, on a blond hill in long grass, a man and a woman mowed in the sunlight, making hay with their scythes as we approached, the woman stooping to gather just as we passed.

From the backseat, unprompted, almost to himself, my father shakily choked out, "Why? Why are we doing this?"

By the time I shifted in my seat to check if I had really heard, he was waving his hands in front of his turned face, as if he were fanning me, fanning me off.

I stuttered out a version of what he had said, miles and miles ago: "A memorial, to try do as memorial, to honor Shmuel…memorial."

"No, no, yes, it's all right. Never mind," he said, in profile, and then, head down, fussed with his bag beside him on the seat. I didn't know what else to say. Other answers would take me a long time to determine.

Shaken a little, I also directed my attention downward, to the backpack on my lap, rooting around and fumbling out a bunch of papers to the floor. Volodya kept his eyes ahead, sparing us in his usual manner, offering a semblance of privacy. I sorted through the spill, sliding the Vishniac photos back in and retrieving the map of Poland. A paper, partly stuck by its inked face to the map's cover, turned out to be the printout that Volodya had dotted over with the rail route back in Munkacs, which seemed ages ago. I hadn't really looked at it since. In the bottom margin, in Volodya's hand, block-printed in Roman letters, were town names I was seeing on road signs now: Biecsz, Gorlice, Grybow. His map was a simple one, the broken red line showing the railway through Slovakia, ending at a blank space southwest of Krakow. In another list, overleaf, I recognized the names of rivers—too many rivers; some we had passed over already, so no longer relevant. The printout wasn't detailed enough to include Oswiecim itself, Auschwitz. The map I unfolded had much more detail and, hard as it was to read in the moving car, I quickly read enough to panic myself: rail lines I hadn't considered before, the area veined with rivers. My uncertainty about finding Shmuel's route returned. So many rail lines, so many waterways. However, there appeared to be only two main ways to go to Auschwitz. Volodya's red line, west but southerly, was one—the way we were traveling now. The other bent north.

Biecsz, Gorlice, Grybow. We were angling back toward the southern route—Volodya's dotted line—after our detour to the Dukla Pass. It was the route he had mapped out back in Munkacs. And this route aligned, generally, with the survivor testimony we had. But what about the rails that went north? Especially those along the Biała River—one of whose northern bridges could reasonably have been the site of Shmuel's escape. Had he considered those? Yet studying the map further, I was overwhelmed by how many divergent railway routes, through many different towns, could be taken from here, all on paths that would end in Auschwitz. As my eye and finger traced the tracks onward, I might as well have been directing surges of panic down my own neural network, a new jolt at every branching. Then I got hold of myself. None of those farther branchings would change our search. Around halfway and a little more, starting from Munkacs, was our touchstone, in investigating the potential locations of Shmuel's attempt—the clues that had been passed along by Zlate Raisel.

But the northern portion of the Biała still looked possible to me, even if it wasn't on Volodya's original dotted line.

Absurd, perhaps, to be desperately questioning the route so far into our journey, but in my English-only bubble I often feared I was missing something crucial. Volodya may have considered and discounted everything that now jumped out at me as possibility. But his natural reserve, and my father as filter for what did come from our guide, made it hard to get a clear notion of the plan, much less refine it. I felt reluctant to have my father translate just then. He seemed fragile.

But I needed to do more than dumb-show signing at Volodya while he drove. I didn't want to look like an idiot by having missed what I'd been told—or feel like an idiot by not saying anything and allowing us to forgo a ready opportunity to examine an alternative. And not exactly an idiot, I realized, but a child, waiting for the adults' revelations again, my current role as an adult contributor, *a* guide if not *the* guide, clearly a sham.

My anxiety mounted as up ahead was an easy way to angle north and intersect the Biała, before backtracking south to follow the tracks along the river. We could check out the bridges of both potential routes *and* return to Volodya's dotted line. And of the many rivers on the way, the Biała felt likely, its bridges few: the rails tended to hug the contours of rivers at a prudent distance from the banks, actually avoiding crossings.

"Dad, could you ask Volodya to pull over a minute?"

"Me too. Maybe there, up ahead." He pointed at some trees, thinking I meant a bathroom break.

"Yeah, a pee would be good, but I want to show Volodya something."

Volodya glanced over, hearing his name. Had he wondered what I had been doing with the map? The last time I'd pored over one in Slovakia he had responded by getting us nearer to tracks—and bridges. I felt he was obliging me then, that he intended most of our close examination to happen later, but I needed those views. For Shmuel, any bridge, including those very ones in Slovakia, might well have given him the idea for his attempt—some change in sound and whatever else. He might have been on the lookout for a long while. These hypotheses, theories about Shmuel's thinking, felt significant to me, almost like moments of divination, of contact somehow. A form of magical thinking, no doubt. Maybe I would see as if through his eyes to feel I had found the place. But then maybe he hadn't gone the way I was urging us to investigate at all.

We stopped and Dad made a bit of a picnic out of it. He always kept bread handy when he traveled, even back home. Bakery bags were stashed in his car: rye bread, often brioche as a treat, but a hedge against hunger went with him at all times. He'd had abundant experience of hunger. So, we were well stocked in the car: bread, cheese, fruit—cherries and grapes particularly—and hard salami. We sat under a tree, passed around bottles of local soda, and ate, a nice change from the intermittent snacking in the car. My father and Volodya chatted some, while I thought about what to say.

"Dad, would you ask Volodya whether we should go north some ways— as far as Gromnik, say? And check out the upper part of the Biała? It isn't the way we thought first, but it's a possible route. It won't take long and, if there's nothing there, we can just come back this way and head south. Should I show him my map?"

My father translated the question, giving little sign of considering what I had asked and why. If anything his tone was a little apologetic. Was he asking Volodya to humor me? Were both of them? Volodya nodded and said something brief, straightforward, neutral. I hardly needed the English. "Yes, north, but no need to go far, a few kilometers. He knows the way." It almost seemed like he was ready for the adjustment—or that it was in his plan from the beginning anyway—another thing I might ask him later, when I felt I could without casting doubt on his stewardship.

We packed up and set off, moving briskly, the road bordered alternatively by fields and woods, and at least one substantial road junction. Then came a number of small towns whose names so taxed pronunciation and memory that even repeating some version of what I had seen on a sign, I couldn't keep the new names in mind long enough to check our location on the map. I gave up and gave myself fully into Volodya's keeping.

In less than half an hour we were near Gromnik, a small town far enough north that it would allow us to explore a fuller length of the Biała. We headed south from there, along the river. For a few minutes there was nothing much to see—road and rail were in sight of each other on and off, but the river didn't converge with the tracks for several kilometers, and when that happened it was only a close proximity that appeared on the crowded map as if it might be more. In fact, I soon understood, observing how map and world corresponded, there was only one obvious bridge-point along that stretch: on a loop of the river somewhere around Zborowice. The countryside looked likely somehow, fields that came right to the river and the rails. He had dropped into a river, swum to a shore, the train meanwhile had backed up, with the polizei shooting. They had killed him on land.

We passed through Zborowice. For stretches, there had been a wall of foliage on one side of the two-lane highway; on the other, river and, at varying distance, rails. After the road's long gradual curve west, the Biała, which had been right beside us, moved away. Beyond a field, a farmhouse on its edge, we could see the bridge, girderless—nothing above the metal sides—and too long to see as a whole from where we pulled over. Approaching on foot, we could see that a lot of the length, a couple hundred feet, was over land—the channel itself wasn't particularly deep and the width couldn't have been more than fifty feet. None of it seemed right. After a few minutes we left.

My father must have been retelling part of the story to Volodya. I heard "Shmuel" and "*most.*" Volodya was saying da, da, *yes, yes, sure, of course, I understand* as we returned to the car. Why was he going over the story now? Volodya had heard it many times, I was sure. Was he emphasizing new details? As we drove off, Dad said something to Volodya and then volunteered a translation before I asked.

"I asked him if the different rivers are all part of the same system, whether all of these are connected. And he said yes."

"Part of the Vistula, I guess," I said. But I suspected he was saying something else. "Dad, are you going to tell me that if we find one river, any river, the Biała here, we can say we have found the place in some way?"

"No, no, we continue looking, of course."

"But if we don't find anything....You remember at Zeyde's funeral there weren't ten men at the graveside, no minyan for praying, and the rabbi pointed at some strangers rows and rows away and said we could count them and do the *brucha*? A crazy technicality to make things seem right. But I'm not ready to give up."

"Jase, we are not giving up. "

"Why don't we say that—for our small *brucha*—that the rivers, all these damn rivers, are connected to each other when we think we have actually found the place—I don't know, to make sure, a guarantee." I was aware that in recommending a blessing I was encroaching on his territory.

Dad smiled a little. "Yes. Then. We should do that, then."

Between Zborowice and Grybow, where we rejoined our main route, Volodya's dotted line, we passed a couple of bridges that were too small to consider. We kept going. In Grybow we found a suitably old bridge on old cement pilings, but high up—as much of the structure over land as water, and the water very shallow. I didn't bother to ask Volodya about the history of water levels. Too much else was obviously wrong. Old buildings stood too near, including a prewar church, and the rail bridge was too much in town. There was no reason even to get out of the car.

Leaving the Biała behind, we headed west toward Nowy Sacz, where two other rivers in the system, the Poprad and the Kamienica, flowed into the larger Dunajec River. We hit the Kamienica first and came across a promising bridge. We got out to take a look. Seeing its old girders got my heart racing—three ancient-looking sections, two old pilings. And then I looked down to the river, what there was of it.

"Ask Volodya whether this would be the standard level, more or less."

Dad translated for him and then for me. "What we have seen, what we will, is about ordinary for this time of year—low water is often the case, in fact. It is a little low now, perhaps."

Volodya continued, and Dad came back to me: "Rarely it's high and then can be too high—four years ago a very big flood."

We debated getting closer, but the problem wasn't only the small, shallow river and low drop to it. The area around the banks, with sizeable trees right to the water's edge, appeared to disqualify the place. We returned to the car. I told myself I hadn't wasted our time and effort by eliminating sites. But I couldn't help thinking that we would have done as well to go straight through the towns noted on the printout, without the detour. I stashed the maps for a while.

We continued west and then south, to my surprise, the one direction I thought would bring us out of range of the route. Dad and Volodya had a brief exchange that sounded informational to me. I got the sense that we weren't traveling *through* but *to* somewhere.

"Dad, what did he say? Aren't we going too far south?"

My father shrugged. "We are just having a look."

As road went to smaller road, the reapers we had seen up on the hill came into my mind. I found myself thinking that we had moved behind the hill, that we were on the other side. I had little idea what that meant, beyond some vague feeling that we had come into the range of the actual lives of people—into essential areas, where events occurred, not the through-lines of roads taking us from one place to another. But, of course, the site of the event we were searching out concerned a transport and the death of someone passing through, someone who had been made a nonperson.

Dad was especially alert; I could feel his hand near my shoulder pulling on the seat as he leaned forward to watch. We drove onto something like a village street—only a few houses—and beyond them was a railroad bridge. Yes, I could see it. And then quickly we drove down another road, half-dirt, that skirted the river, and stopped beside low scrub ground. The anticipation that had built in me, really against my will—too far south, surely—dissipated quickly as we approached. I gestured at the water, again shallow. I turned toward Volodya. "What river?"

"Poprad," he said.

I recalled it from my map reading. The Poprad formed part of the border with Slovakia before bending north, the railroad tracks with it, and emptying into the larger Dunajec, not far from where we were. More than intuition made us doubtful: no jumping off and swimming to a field here. Too shallow, and the width of the bed, as defined by the spread of stones and the markings on the low banks, seemed to guarantee that judgment, whatever the modest variations over seasons or years. And was the bridge long enough? I remained unsure of length as a criterion: there was something about the timing of the leap that I hadn't quite articulated, not even to myself. We returned to the car and rejoined the main road north.

Their talk had become more sporadic as we made our way through Novy Sacz. Did my dad wonder and worry as I did that no place would fit the description, such as it was? Yet he seemed easier with things at this point, calm since his small outcry. When he and Volodya did speak, I was alerted by Shmuel's name and strained to pick up Russian words I might understand: *gora* (mountain), *goroda* (towns), *mnogo* (many). At first I thought they were consulting about directions, but then I recognized that my father was retelling parts of the story. Hadn't it been near mountains that those on the transport got some idea of where they had been, that had confirmed that notion of midway? Who had told me that?

There were mountains ahead and, suddenly, a wide river and a long bridge, three sections of box girders on tapered cement-block footings. There were substantial fields on both banks, and on one tidied area on the eastern side a soccer game was in progress. Behind them was a church dome and another steeple, the town's edge.

I retrieved the camera from the pack at my feet. I'd heard no *most* from Volodya; no one played lookout, sang out with a sighting. It was a big bridge compared to what we'd seen, so there was no need to say a thing. We simply drove to where we could get close, and then it was easy to get onto the bridge itself and walk the checker-plate steel the rails were anchored to, and to look north and south over the sides.

Dad paced with Volodya toward one end and then the other. I followed, filming on and off. They stopped at intervals, heads leaning together. My dad called out to me with some detail from time to time, his own or Volodya's. Looking over the side, they gauged the drop to the water—fifteen meters. Then more estimates: the length of the bridge was two or three hundred meters. Length meant more time. But a moving train and those girders. How could Shmuel jump through? As if they had read my mind, my dad said, "Volodya says the trains were heavy. In all bridges they were going slowly, this was deliberate. Very slow on a bridge like this."

That hadn't occurred to me. Shmuel would not have had to leap immediately; he would have had the chance to judge, to hang there and time his jump. The trains were so overloaded, and the bridge wasn't new even then. We saw a rail embossed with the date 1929 and could see old foundry markings on the girders.

"The name, Dad, ask Volodya, the name of river."

"He says it is the Dunajec."

"And that's Nowy Sacz, the buildings over there?"

"*Da*," said Volodya, and repeated both names, properly pronounced.

Letting them walk on, I stopped, filming around me and for a moment aiming the lens straight down the bridge, so that the geometry of the view made it feel like a tunnel or a mine shaft, the girders running together and giving an illusion of solidity. I moved to one side and caught sight of something at the east end of the bridge—a cross on an upright stone, some kind of memorial. Before I could inspect it, Dad called, moving toward me. I turned so that he was in the tunnel of the lens. He was speaking to me, and not quite to me, but to the camera.

"Of all the bridges we have seen, of the few bridges we have seen, this one seems the most likely because the water is deep enough and the bridge is an old bridge—nothing here was touched or changed, and the fact that there is so much wide-open space."

His words were an announcement of what we knew already: what was in the story and what was around us. A long bridge, a deep-enough river, a large stretch of fields. All necessary and sufficient for Shmuel to have been able to leap and then swim to where he could run.

They returned to the east end of the bridge, Volodya walking with his hands clasped behind him. I kept filming them as Volodya stepped toward my father, speaking. Dad translated, almost inattentively, not assessing as he had been moments ago, when he was entirely with Volodya, speaking back and forth, passing on calculations. This time he seemed a little distracted as he simply relayed information.

Most kolejowy na Dunajcu: *the railroad bridge over the Dunajec River, near Nowy Sacz, Poland*

"Volodya says there's a curve—you see down there. He could have looked maybe ahead and seen there was a bridge."

Was Volodya deducing along with us or did he have a theory before we got to this place, and didn't want to lead us too much?

"Volodya says it's about 180 kilometers to Auschwitz from here."

Even slowed by weight and hills, the train could still have arrived from here in the morning, the same day anyhow, certainly, however long it took: three hours, four hours, five hours. Now inside that wagon they would have surely been arguing; now Zlate Raisel would have tried to stop him.

"It's halfway. About halfway," Dad said.

Suddenly I thought something had gone wrong with the camera, but, no, the light had dipped, the bright sky clouding over.

"Volodya says the rivers from here are not this big."

Had Shmuel seen these mountains, the encircling mountains, before he saw the river and field? In which direction would he have been looking? At what point could he have seen them?

Dad was looking up at the peaks and out along the river.

"Volodya was saying what you were saying before," he said, "almost verbatim repeating. We put together small, little details, this and that, to come to some kind of understanding, some knowledge."

I could feel my father beginning to enter his grief.

"And also again I repeat the idea that the territory is a place you could jump out. He contemplated that this was a place you could run someplace."

I was caught up in the moment, but slowly, secondhand, or even at further remove, through the tunnel of a lens, dodging behind the viewfinder. And my father, in spite of the rising emotion, was tamping down his feelings in front of the camera too. Even the opportunity of using that grief toward the higher purpose of instructing humanity about the Holocaust wasn't enough for him to expose himself just then. The specifics of scene before us—bridge, mountains, river, field, and, reconstructed in mind, the leap and swim and flight from gunfire—weren't something to be retold. It wasn't material for a lesson.

He wanted me to film, though. I held to that idea, the duty that allowed me to stay behind the camera, to continue the dodge. I could see struggle in his facial muscles. Again, he was speaking, to me and not to me—to himself mostly.

"Where they are playing soccer, that is maybe where he was shot," he said.

I checked the direction of the current. It was possible. Shmuel could have reached that place on that riverbank. It could have been in the field. If it were here.

My father stared down at the river. I saw that something was happening to him. He was beginning to believe, a belief that was more than the sum of our calculations. And what did I feel? What I had hoped for all along was an undeniable, unreasonable sense that we had arrived at the place—like the sudden pluck on the dowser's wand, the apparitional chill. Not something I sought but something that came for me. Even if, at the same time, I understood that such a thing was ridiculous. And I continued, my face behind the camera, diverting myself from belief by *thinking* about belief, about the place, about what I should feel, while at the same time fearing that I would not feel. I was veering away from what was before me: my father believing it was the bridge of our search, starting to imagine his brother in those final moments. I saw it in the change in his face as he looked at the river, at the field, and then back at me.

As I had feared earlier on the trip, I was now afraid I would not respond to him properly, that things stood in the way—resentments of my own, resentments of the story itself, his story and what it had made of him. And what it required of me, of us, of everyone close to him.

"The sky," he said. "It's raining." Dappling the dust on the rails, the scattered drops joined to fill the blank spaces, deepening the rust color of the surfaces of steel plate and rail.

Volodya said something.

Dad said, "It's like crying."

But then he couldn't speak, beginning to cry himself. I stepped closer, still with the camera between us, ready to apologize for wanting to know my uncle, though really for my part in bringing my father to this place.

"Dad, you knew him, you don't have to imagine the man. I try to imagine him from what he did...this courage."

My uncle who was like me somehow. Dad had said so. Yet it was especially hard to see myself in him here in what he did. I did believe that this was the bridge. I still do. But any apology would be an evasion. I wasn't sorry to have what I could of my uncle—but it was my father I wanted to

*Volodya and Dad walking back and forth on the bridge, talking about the surroundings in light of the story we had*

know, to find a way to love him more freely and set aside whatever it was that held me back. And still did.

And hadn't I wanted exactly this, to be here, both of us feeling whatever we felt? A moment not to be folded into a story, not an illustration of anything, but simply what it was—what we were. (Though I tell it now to make some kind of story, to illustrate something.)

"No, no, it's all right," he said. And he turned from me and wept.

*Can we edit this out?* I thought, my oddest thought yet. Odder still was how I stayed behind the camera, as if it were required of me. My excuse, my veering, was my father's sense that we were recording something significant for an audience of more than ourselves. But this was for ourselves, too; we would see it all again, and neither of us would want this moment preserved, neither of us would want to see later, ever, my father breaking down like this.

"We should go," he said. Several times over.

This wasn't for preserving. I had to stop filming. I had to stop thinking. I knew I should go to him—this man with his own story, who had given

*Volodya waiting as Dad begins to tell me what he thinks about this river and the fields around it*

me so much—and much that I hadn't wanted. So often I'd been angry with him, but this was somewhere I had always needed to be, where nothing could be rehearsed; not his feeling, not mine. I felt for him, and I did put aside the camera, though I was a beat or two late. A beat or two only in the world outside my own head, but I knew, I was aware, that I was no cameraman. I was this man's son and should go to him and put an arm around his shoulder and walk with him a little while. And I did. I went to him, but I was late by my own measure. I told myself that he wouldn't notice, that he never much managed to follow my inner workings, that he would say to himself, and to anyone to whom he might talk about this, that his son comforted him on the bridge when he could almost see what had happened there to his brother. I told myself that he wouldn't truly notice my delay and that for some brief moments we were together there, when there was no story about his brother's desperate courage, no story at all.

We walked up and down a while together. The rain stuttered intermittently, as if about to start in earnest and then stopping.

We honored Shmuel. And what does that mean but to make this effort as if he could see us, or to pretend that he could? To pretend and to sacrifice. We gave up our time, and it cost us time and money and effort. It *was* a sacrifice, which gave the gesture meaning. It was an abyss gesture, as if we had thrown something we will never have again into the deaf, blind, scentless, and untouchable darkness of afterlife. We threw time into nothingness so that Shmuel might have value again, as if we could graft onto his life something of ours, what ours is made of—time, the time he did not have, that was taken from him. And we did this as if he could hear, as if he could know. We took it on ourselves—by assignment of will—to be the priests of this burning of time; we are the only ones who can go into the holy of holies and say the name.

We commemorated, sacrificed time, made the effort, and measured that effort by the ache of travel, in weariness. And we did it all as if someone beyond earth—a God, the dead themselves—could hear; as if there could be permanent value, seconded, ratified, established by the very universe itself; as if what's on earth is heard or seen elsewhere, beyond death and dying. Because, by definition, God doesn't die, and if the dead can hear then they don't die either, and they can help us hold on to what matters, just by listening, listening and simply nodding. They don't even have to give a sign, though a sign would be nice. Don't let me stop you, Uncle Shmuel, sign away! Though something more than rain, please. And the incidental dimming and return of the light.

Light itself alone will probably have to do. The solace of physics: the way light travels, the light of the sun, any light reflected off a scene, off people and things. I've read that if you could get out beyond the light reflected off some moment, any moment—the moment Shmuel leapt—if you could penetrate the folds of space-time or were already out there, looking back, you could see what happened, exactly where the murder was. Is. In fact, the light of that is still traveling outward, if not forever, then for the duration of the universe, as long as what is, is. As close to forever as can be, that traveling to the end of time, to the end of light.

After I walked with him a little, my arm around his shoulder, my father gathered himself. As at the Munkacs graveyard, he asked for some time by himself, and I let him walk on his own a while. Volodya waited a few yards off, mid-bridge, his hands clasped in front of him. I went to the other end to see about that stone with the cross. It appeared to be some small garden of remembrance fenced off behind iron pickets down the slope, the large rectangular stone in the center. The plaque in Polish words had recognizable roots: *Hitlerowskiego barbarzynstwa, okupach* 1939–1945—Hitler's barbarism during the occupation. The stele commemorated 180 local victims, including a military doctor, executed here, who had been the first. Not a grave, but a place of execution and of commemoration. Rationally, this should have meant nothing to our search, to the bridge being Shmuel's bridge, and yet it did not feel as if it meant nothing. I would learn years later that there had been some fifteen thousand Jews, uncommemorated, who slept on these fields by the bridge in August 1942. Already brutalized in the Nowy Sacz ghetto, they had waited here to be loaded into trains to the Belzec death camp.

The bridge had no name and was identified only as *most kolejowy*—railway bridge—Nowy Sacz. As we drove away, Volodya commented on how the sun had come out.

"Volodya says that when we were on the bridge it got dark and rained but now look how the sun is out. We can a little be at peace now."

And it struck me—was it possible that Volodya had wanted to find the bridge almost as much as we did? That he wanted to give Dad that bridge? And I understood then what my father sought from others, others who hadn't been entangled in the daily addition and subtraction of a life close to him. A generous day or two costs less, can be given more freely than generous years, and whatever connection may follow will be outside of that daily tangle that mounts into years. My father wanted such things, such sympathies, from others, and believed he could have them, could identify those who might give them. His safety and survival had relied on that ability. And for his part, Volodya had, from my father, not just his charm but the intimate fellowship of travel, those moments that come without having to travel, paired, to the very end of all travel. It was a one-night stand of a kind that must occasionally happen where there is real tenderness, freely given because it will not be required long, may not be possible again. A gift of height and not length.

We continued for several hours on the road. We were a little tired, but not so much that the high-frequency current among us had hummed out. There were other bridges and rivers on our way, but much too far west according to the narrative we steered by. We stopped briefly at a few anyway, for comparison, as my father said to the camera, and simply viewed others in passing from the car: in Mszana Dolna a rail bridge on the Mszunka River; in Marki and Zaryte and Rabka, all on the Raba; in Jordanow on the Skawa; two around Juszczyn. All were too small, we said, and too far. Too close to the last rivers that lay ahead of us—the branching at Auschwitz of the Vistula and its tributary, the Sola, the rivers that had received such a quantity of ash.

# 10

*Your pardon, Lilly, anyway*
*for bringing these things up again,*
*also for retelling*
*what you know better than anyone,*
*out here where others listen,*
*as if it were something of my own.*

AUSCHWITZ. Even with our early arrival, not yet nine, people had already gathered, preparing for the camp, now the museum. In the parking lot, we made our way past knots of visitors already grouped around guides by language, getting acquainted and making a start. I could pick out a word here and there, and with the context so evident, it was easy to gather a sense of the subject, most of it introductory. This was the beginning of the tour; this was the morning, a pleasant Saturday morning, the first of June. I heard the Spanish *mil novecientos cuarenta y uno*. 1941. That guide was starting with the establishment of the main camp on the site of former Polish army barracks. The first prisoners, the first slave laborers, most of the first murdered, were Soviet soldiers.

The next word I caught, *Lehrspruch*, I made a guess at—and my father confirmed: a pithy saying, an aphorism. Chilling to hear the sound of German, though. The guide, a thirtyish woman with sandy hair and turned-up nose, Polish by the look of her, was pointing at the iron arch above the main gate as she introduced a solemn group of young Germans to its infamous slogan, *Arbeit Macht Frei*. Not the first manifestation of evil the inmates would have had in that language. I had the thought that perhaps these young people were German-speaking Swiss—as if that were a comfort—then dismissed the idea for the silliness it was, part of a set of odd mental adjustments to entering. As was the notion that this arch was not the gate to hell for those of "ours," as Shmuel would have entered, as Lilly did, at the so-called ramp in Auschwitz II, Auschwitz-Birkenau. So this original part of the camp complex would be a kind of prelude, a preparation, as it was during the war in a way, for the "improved" versions in that expanded camp at Birkenau, a couple of miles away, which we would visit after lunch.

As we moved through the gate, I caught the entirety of a French phrase: *Ici les Juifs et autres.* Here Jews and others. We had studied enough to know enough, to believe we didn't need a guide. Volodya kept close to my father and always seemed to understand when to give us both some space—though at this moment we were hard to read, even to ourselves. I was entirely uncertain of my father's mood. We were both a little wrung out from the past couple of days, and tense too. The search for the bridge. The bridge itself. I felt especially nervous. Over what, though? It could hardly be this camp. After all that I had read, the histories, the memoirs. What was at issue here? What we had hoped for from the trip, at least in terms of the physical destination, our personal ceremony, had been performed— unreasonable intuition and logical confidence, based on evidence, assured us we had found what we were looking for.

And to continue here, to Auschwitz, would complete the journey in some sense—not Shmuel's alone, not Shmuel's at all, really. Others had to be honored too, with deliberate efforts at memory, at placing into memory, at underscoring; they were no less deserving of the gesture for not being connected to us by family. Most who come here must feel that something is owed those who died here, the Jews and others. I badly wanted our trip, and this visit, to have meaning that I could understand and express. But at Auschwitz, as in other places we had been, this proved difficult. Easy to say we honored the memory and by remembering, helped prevent. And perhaps the memories and monuments had been a bulwark, but there was plenty of evidence to the contrary.

At his side, Volodya had been speaking at some length to my father,

*At the gate of Auschwitz I, under the notorious sign that translates "Work Will Make You Free." The fact that the "B" was inverted by the Jewish craftsman who made it has been taken as an act of resistance.*

who turned to me and said, "I wish you could hear what he says—that it's jealousy, the hate for Jews. His grandfather had a store and knew Jewish people and had respect for their intelligence, and saw how the others were against them. And before he was talking about Israel, so sensible—and not for show for me. No, very genuine."

As the groups flowed into a modest crowd that siphoned through the gate, I noticed the tiny dance of courtesies here and there, people deferring to one another, one letting another go first—here was the spell—civility, at minimum—to pray for, that it would hold. An elderly woman dropped her bag and several people stopped to help. A slight gesture, and my attentiveness to it mostly an example of my desperate search for the antidote to the poisonous aura of cruelty radiating from this ground. So much more of that we would meet in artifact during the hours to come. So, I was concentrating on small kindnesses practiced, stretching that into a sort of symbolic recognition that others are like us, feel as we do, that there are no real others. That was the hard part to keep in mind, verging on paradox—that we, who stood there prepared to have our attention directed at horrors, were like all of the people who were here, not just the ones we had come to mourn. We were like some of them in ways that must be recognized and guarded against. Not monsters, those men and women in the military uniforms. Monsters can be too easily dismissed. Monsters are part of a game, the "not us," the ready frisson.

I was suddenly surprised by Hebrew, coming from a young couple up ahead to the left. They had already passed through the gate: a tall woman in a khaki skirt, pale legs, hair pulled back in a ponytail, and a shorter man, much darker. Why was I surprised? I looked back to see if my father had heard, but he was talking with Volodya. My relief made me realize how badly I wanted to avoid my father's collecting people, or his practicing languages. Maybe he wouldn't have, not here. In any case, the couple moved ahead briskly down the path. I slowed so we three could tour more or less together.

The first jolt on entering the camp was the aesthetics, the groomed pebble path, the old red-brick buildings. "Like a college," I hissed at my father, hating that I thought that. He looked faintly alarmed at my tone, which made me aware of it. I associated anger with those at further remove from the Shoah than I was, the sort of unspecific response of some American Jews I'd encountered. That anger, like others, covered for a range of possible emotions.

Part of my reaction was to the color, the natural liveliness of color, even the muted old brick, rich with texture, and the ordinary greenery. As with Munkacs, so many of the images I had seen were black and white. Here was the continuing contemporary life of grass and trees in the bright light of a summer day, all of which made the place seem less than what it had been. One quickly got used to the cement posts with the many strands of barbed wire that screened or backed every view. And the site seemed so small, the diminished proportions of a childhood neighborhood revisited. The sign over the gate offered one kind of irony; the camp beyond seemed to participate in another sort.

The Auschwitz orchestra had played beside this gate, with an emphasis on marching music to usher the slave laborers out and in, though entertainment for the attending guards too, I supposed. We headed to the "blocks," the barrack buildings that housed exhibits, much of the exhibited material brought here from Birkenau. We meandered through, typically separating within each building to take our own paths through and rejoining to proceed to another barracks.

Block 4 was where all tours began and was a little crowded at the entrance, so we deferred and walked down to Block 7: "Daily Life." Sometimes we allowed our progress to be dictated by the several groups circulating, all relatively small, no more than six or seven people at most. But at any delay at an entrance, we exchanged a look and moved on. Occasionally we eavesdropped a little: I by the rim of a small English-speaking group that intersected with us now and then; my father by any group. But it wasn't particularly crowded overall. Auschwitz had not yet become the destination it is—more than two million visitors a year now—a mainstay of the phenomenon of "dark tourism."

The corridor of Block 7 was lined with black-and-white photographs of Polish political prisoners, whose striped uniforms would have carried a red triangle. Taken on entry to the camp, these head shots had captions that noted the number, date of arrival, date of death, and former professions of the prisoners. Some had the star that marked them as Jews; for them arrival and death dates were invariably close. I noted some odd translations in the explanatory signs; typos, too. One of the captions had nationality as *Polka* instead of *Polak*. Small things, but carelessness here that troubled me.

The exhibits had to manage a constant tension between the massive numbers and the effort to represent individuals. So these pictures, so these faces. I heard a psychologist say once that no one can truly multitask, that what happens is a rapid alternation in attention, which flashes from one thing to another. Here the observer is brought into an exhausting back-and-forth between the incomprehensible numbers and whatever sense of person and personal fate could be communicated.

I didn't have to remind myself that this was a Polish museum, and that the Poles had suffered too. The fact was emphatic in Auschwitz I. It represented another difficult balance, not necessarily for the museum but for me, who kept having the ungenerous but true thought that many Poles disliked Jews. But how many and how much? I was looking for the text, for the sign, that would say that there had been forced and unforced cooperation with the Germans, and how much of each. What did the Polish train driver feel as he drew his thumb across his throat in Lanzmann's *Shoah*? Was he signaling a warning to the Jews, already too late, or was there cruelty in the gesture? No pure hearts, no pure race, no pure truth.

Meanwhile, flowing beneath my thoughts were questions: What should I feel about all of this? What were my flares of anger a cover for? Perhaps not knowing what to feel, I suspected I didn't feel enough. And anger rose so sharply defined; being merely bewildered seemed like a failure.

We moved toward Block 5. My father had said little from the beginning of the day. He appeared a little dazed, some drift in his walk that had him looking his age now and then, in a way his vigor typically masked, and now the smallest of stumbles.

"Dad, how are you doing? Are you all right?"

I was aware of at least one possible component of his feelings, one respect in which he was overmatched by what we faced. He had often mentioned that his experience was no way as difficult as those at Auschwitz. He stressed always his luck, downplaying the courage and resourcefulness that must have figured into his survival.

"Fine, fine," he said. "Just a bigger stone or something." He paused for a moment and continued. "You know I have been here before once."

"I'm not sure I did. Maybe. It wasn't when you went to Munkacs with Mom?"

"No, by myself. I joined a group of Italians in the hotel, but I nearly had to leave as soon as we came here. I felt sick."

"Did you get to Birkenau?"

"Oh, yes, I went, and everywhere there I made kaddish for the dead, I said the names of my family, everyone I could remember, I said kaddish for them."

Over the doorway to Block 5 was the legend "Material Proof of Crimes" in both Polish and English. Here were the cases that displayed the granary heaps of eyeglasses, shoes, pots and pans, valises, artificial limbs, dolls, and children's clothes. Everything here was meant as metonymy for absence, loss, murder. All of it, the remnants of remnants, had been collected at the end from Birkenau, from an area called Kanada, which housed possessions thieved from the million-plus of the transports who had been through here, murdered and burned. Some of these objects must have belonged to those who had survived, the barest sample themselves, the smallest of remnants.

These objects remained of the rest: the countless (well, counted some-where) bales of hair sent to Germany for stuffing mattresses and weaving into uniforms and socks, artificial limbs sent to German veterans and ci-vilians. Samplings, remnants of remnants—what did all of this amount to, several weeks' or less worth of the spoils from the trains, this "material proof" secured by the Russian liberators and brought here? Or was it the Poles who transferred the objects, the ex-prisoners of the grassroots group that started the museum even before a restored Polish government provided funds for it?

This abundance of samples had become emblems to remind and dis-place, like the photos that replace memories. By means of the artifacts, my father would feel that his experience was something less, diminished by these representations that the world had ratified. All the peculiar stories of survival from elsewhere, like the uneven shapes of the individual scars, were replaced by these objects. I thought of my father's nose with a wing sewn back on by a shoemaker, severed by shrapnel from an Allied bomb. Part of his Holocaust. What was preserved here was offered as necessary shorthand: hair, eyeglasses, hairbrushes, pans, shoes. Intended for a mo-ment of focus, destined for the effort to inspire, but inspiring what? Diz-zying to think of how responses must vary according to individuals. It all depended: grief maybe, anger, perhaps an empty deference.

As I went by the display cases, I thought I could identify, in myself and others around me, something like an emotional catatonia, so many dif-ferent calls on feeling that a paralysis ensued. The state breached by some stimulus or other to which one is particularly vulnerable. For me, I had to hold back tears on seeing a piece of paper, an intake record of a person whose crime was sheltering Jews. A woman whose path crossed ours sev-eral times with a fixed blank expression, contorted into tears as she looked down at a child's sweater.

I rejoined my father and walked with him through the corridors of display, stopping to gaze through our reflections at shoes, banks and shoals of them. How could I know what he was feeling at any specific moment? Yet I believed I did, in part. How could there not be that one familiar note, that self-diminution, in the face of the extremity of suffer-ing symboled here? But his had to have been a different sort from that of a casual observer. Of course, I thought of Lilly when we were there, and I found myself returning to one particular occasion at her home in Brooklyn.

I had come to Canarsie to see her around 1993, as she had recently, and dramatically, begun to speak about her experiences. She had agreed to sit for a taped interview. I had been writing poems of a nonfictional sort, drawn from survivor testimony in which she figured, and I wanted to be sure about things she told me. I tried to get her words right, and I would later fact-check, though guiltily, as thoroughly as I could, whatever I could, in histories and various survivor memoirs. Lilly was the one who had first made me aware of the "Auschwitz lovers," Edek and Mala. On several occasions after my discussions with her I had the singular experience of reading a well-known memoir and coming upon an incident she had related to me, literally seen from a different angle but unmistakably the same event. Once, the shared anecdote concerned an awful beating at roll call administered by the head of the women's camp, who had dragged a woman around by a belt leashed around her neck, choking and clubbing her almost to death.

In Lilly and Harry's living room, we three drank some tea before Lilly and I got started, a visit and a chance for the two of us to settle in. I'd asked her to tell me when she was ready. So, in the briefest of pauses, after an exchange of family news, she abruptly got up to lead the way into the back room where we were to talk. I rose to follow, and as I turned to take up a pad and a small tape recorder from a side table, Harry stopped me. "If you would like to know about the Hungarian labor battalions, I could tell you..." Lilly, a few steps ahead, whirled on him, interrupting, "Auschwitz, Herschel, Auschwitz." She sailed on, him silenced, me following.

I understood that there was hierarchy among the survivors, which could hardly have come only from the survivors themselves. The repetitions of mass media had figured in the assignment of notoriety, of primacy, by others. Auschwitz furnished reliable barbarism; its associated objects and setting, its tropes, were familiar now. In the labor battalions, though, the experience depended on who was in immediate authority; that is, how anti-Semitic the Hungarian overseers were and what the labor was and where it was performed. Conditions on the Russian front were especially harsh: the brutality of the labor battalions could, in fact, be similar to that of Auschwitz. Of some hundred and thirty thousand men sent east, very few had returned. (But I have just done the very thing I object to: entering into the business of the rankings, arguing for the validity of one corner of hell by comparing it to another.) And how did my father himself really assess being hunted, betrayed, put under threat of death so constantly? Did he truly always set his experience beside this epitome of suffering, weighing it, and finding it wanting? Was that why—or was it one of the reasons—he stopped telling about some things, like the beatings in the transit camp?

Block 11 was for punishment, the death block. The main floor had the Gestapo courtroom with a long table, two chairs on one side, nine on the other, next to the rooms where prisoners stripped for execution in the space between Blocks 10 and 11. Beneath our feet were the basement rooms that had been used for smothering, starving, and the initial experimentation with Zyklon B gas; also, tiny chambers where prisoners were forced to stand all night and then, by day, be worked to a death hastened by this enhanced exhaustion.

We had entered on the heels of a small group of French speakers, and I could make out some words and names, including a *pere*, a priest, Maximilian Kohlbe. The guide spoke of how Kohlbe, since canonized, spent three weeks in *cellule dix-huit*, cell 18, without food, having asked the SS to allow him to trade places with a Pole who had a family. They took him out to kill him in the end. As we sidled past, I heard more names, other words easily recognized, which opened on other events: Edek and Mala, *les amoureux d'Auschwitz*. The lovers of Auschwitz had been imprisoned here, questioned here, and had made their marks on the walls of their cells. Did my father know that story? He didn't.

"I will tell you later, at Birkenau," I said to him. "Lilly was there at the execution. It happened at Birkenau; they escaped from there. I will tell you there."

He looked at me strangely and I knew, again, my tone had been peculiar. Perhaps our avoidance was some sort of decorum, but none of us attempted to go down to the cells, though we did go to the execution wall. Volodya brought up the rear, having dropped back a few steps during my exchange with Dad, acute as ever in hearing the distinctions in speech, no matter the language.

As we left Block 11 and turned toward the gate into the execution yard, the Israeli couple passed us, pale her and dark him, striding in the direction of the main entrance and the bus to Birkenau. Had they already seen what they wanted to? Compact as the place was, I wondered at their speed. We entered the yard. At the north end was the wall, porous looking, made of some substance to absorb ricochet, though firing squads had not operated here, but bullets to the back of the head. Thousands died here, most of them Polish. The windows that overlooked the yard from the neighboring barracks were boarded. I looked up at the upper floors of Block 10, where Nazi doctors had experimented on Jewish women—where they lost breasts and wombs, where they were irradiated, where they lost their lives.

After doubling back to Block 4, for the overview of the whole dreadful process of extermination, we walked on to the national exhibits, the most lightly attended area of the camp thus far, and quickly went in and out of several: Jews, citizens again, commemorated by nation. I was reminded that where the Soviets had had influence there was an emphasis on nation and a reticence about Jews: I had been to Sachsenhausen in the nineties, soon after the fall of the Berlin Wall, with my friend David. That camp, which did focus on political prisoners, had nevertheless imprisoned many Jews, yet I don't remember the word "Jew" appearing once. All victims were identified as antifascists. In Ravensbruck, which we visited on the same trip, signs demonstrated a similar reluctance to mention Jews, sorting inmates by nationality. And Russian troops were still there then, waiting for accommodations to be built back home so they could return.

At Block 18, the Hungarians had their complex and disgraceful history muted to a virtual whisper. The Germans were blamed and there were names, names on walls, some four hundred and thirty thousand, there would have to be, wouldn't there? I circulated, glancing around, only half concentrating, standing before a column of the letter S, and...

"Dad, Dad, come here." I was aware that I had shouted. The few other people in the room whipped heads around. He came over quickly.

"Look." I pointed at the name, the Hungarian version, not Shmiel or Shmuel, but Samuel. "See, Samuel Steinberger. From the transport list. Whether they arrived or not." We stood and stared, took pictures. But what we were seeing? That he had been duly registered by those who murdered him, which allowed for him, his name, to be on this wall.

I took my father's arm and we walked out. One more building. I planned to look in at the French exhibition, to see whether it mentioned that their own police had rounded up prisoners for transport, though in many cases they avoided deporting their own citizens by first revoking the Jews' citizenship. My father stopped outside this less-trafficked area and said, "I'm going to be here." It was midmorning. He took a prayer book from his small satchel and, facing east beside a barrack's steps, started praying. Here at Auschwitz, on Shabbat. I left him to it, to address God at Auschwitz. And left the old argument we'd often had on the subject for another time.

I continued, visited by the sense that there was something deeply suspect about the whole exercise. Random segments of overheard narration seemed misleading or incomplete in some way. But how could every utterance be comprehensive, given what needed to be comprehended? Sometimes the signage of the displays felt wrong. At the same time, I was acutely aware that no way existed to make it right. At the heart of everything were the unwilling subjects of the photographs, tortured and starved, skeletal, deformed by surgery. One photograph of a naked woman, blown up to poster size, had what looked at first glance like a large smudge over one breast. I realized that the smudge was what had been done to the breast and not the photograph.

The prisoners themselves had smuggled out images of actual gassing— for all the good that did. And the liberators, requiring proof, also took photos. Had anyone asked the prisoners? The heaped dead, of course, could not have consented. But the living—their wills had been overwhelmed by so much, the least of which would have been the horror and sympathy accompanying their liberators' cameras, however that might have differed from the cold voyeurism of the Nazi documenters. The prisoners' absolute subjection, Jews and others, was unsettling and kept surfacing in my mind as I went through the buildings. Somewhere there had been a brothel established by the Nazis in one of these blocks. Knowing what humans are, there must have been pictures taken there. But not of Jews, neither as clients nor workers, which was forbidden by the Nazis, though who could say absolutely, none, never?

The last place we visited was the gas chamber, just outside the camp proper, very near the commandant's house. It had been a converted garage. As we approached, four or five people stood outside, addressed in Polish-accented English by their guide, who would orient them here as there was supposed to be silence inside the chamber itself and the crematorium area. This building had been converted again into an SS bomb shelter after the improved chambers, four of them, had been put into service in Birkenau. Here they had kept truck engines running to cover the screams of the dying. That noise was why they had built the chambers and crematoria in Birkenau underground.

As we walked around the group and entered, I learned that the space had been restored, with its original equipment, by Polish ex-prisoners. That stuck with me for the sheer oddness of imagining such restoration. Inside, I stared at the marks on the walls. I had read much about the awful struggle of those dying from Zyklon B poisoning, but it was strange to feel suddenly that I couldn't know for certain what marks were made by what human activity. Even wondering at that seemed a peculiar misdirection, another example for me, perhaps, of a misplaced impulse toward precision. I distracted myself from all that I could not understand by occupying myself with small points, small truths, as if they could accumulate into larger ones, and in the face of insoluble mysteries—like the root of human evil.

We lunched quickly out of the car, heavy on bread and cheese washed down with bottled water, everything sun-warm. We sat inside with the doors open, watching the comings and goings. The numbers of arrivals, which had climbed during the morning, had tapered off a little, and it appeared that few who had exited with us were going toward the bus to Birkenau, which confirmed our decision to take it. A number of cars were turning in the direction of the town.

"Hey, Dad, see those cars leaving? You think they are going to eat in Oswiecim?"

Our own simple dining arrangements suddenly felt virtuous to me. I tried to imagine sitting in a restaurant on a lunch break between Auschwitz I and Auschwitz II.

He looked toward the exit. "I suppose, yes, probably." He brushed some crumbs off his palms. He said something to Volodya and then to me.

"Are we almost ready?"

"*Poshli*, then?" I asked him.

He smiled a little, "*Poshli*."

So the bus shuttled the three of us, and only a handful more, the couple of miles from Auschwitz I, down a nondescript country road, one of whose curves swung us into a view of the cement fence posts and barbed wire and wooden guard towers.

Set down by the front gate, we faced the entrance, an oblong brick building crested with a guardhouse, which now featured a bookstore and restrooms at street level. Tracks led straight through an archway into the camp. A couple of hundred yards ahead of us lay the area of the infamous ramp, so-called, the extension of the rails added in 1944 to accommodate the anticipated mass of Hungarian Jews. Approximately half a million souls had been expected. We entered through the pedestrian gate to the left of the rails.

After the bus ride and the close-set brick enclosures of the main camp, this sudden vista was like looking out over an ocean, as if the viewer's very self could be thinned over the expanse by the act of viewing. The lines of the rails and the lines of barbed wire inscribing the air, bordering and segmenting the flat ground, were like an exercise in plane geometry, the world as schematics. I had the odd first thought that it didn't seem much different from its diagram, in two dimensions on paper. I had looked so often at aerial views and maps, that their afterimage seemed before me still. I had the sectors pretty well memorized, especially around 1944. To the right were the rectangles of the men's camp, with the Roma family camp next to it; to the left, the women's camp, where Lilly had been.

*Volodya and my father walking and talking at Auschwitz II, Birkenau*

To say "left" and "right" here was to say the words for life or death. *Links* or *rechts*, the SS doctors would say on the ramp—not really a ramp, merely the place of unloading and sifting. First the men were separated from the women and young children. Then the further division: the uniformed men, all doctors who performed the selections, sent most to the right, to their deaths. Those they certified as healthy and strong enough to live for a time as slave laborers they sent left.

The rails continued to the western end of the camp, to the gas chambers and crematoria, to Kanada and its warehouses, to the ash ponds, but also to the place of delousing and hair-shearing. Perhaps seventy yards ahead of us began the path Lilly had taken through Auschwitz-Birkenau, chosen for life along with her sisters. They had been sent in one direction and their mother, father, and brothers had been sent another. I knew the number of their barracks in the women's camp and intended to find it. Though we had gone beyond Shmuel's journey, and my father's, it was not so much beyond. Shmuel's name was on a wall in the museum barracks. Many of my family died here, names that my father could name, had named for me, those I would never have the chance to know beyond their names. Doubtless there had been some of my mother's family, those who had remained in Europe, but those names would have been unknown, probably even to my maternal grandparents.

We would soon be following the path of Lilly and her sisters, tracks to the main road, the *Lagerstrasse*, down to the "sauna" building where they had been shaved and shorn of all hair and deloused. I stopped for a moment. Dad and Volodya lagged a few paces behind me, conversing. My father spoke mostly, his voice faintly instructional, expository—something about Budapest and Csepel. I thought perhaps he was saying where he had been when the Munkacs transports were arriving. We didn't go down the *Lagerstrasse*, though, but turned to the north without discussion to several restored barracks, dutifully following the standard route for visitors. The barracks, originally prefabricated horse stables, had been part of a quarantine area. Most of the rest of the buildings had been destroyed after the abandonment of the camp. The largest number had been disassembled by the Poles, who needed building materials for postwar reconstruction. Even these reconstituted ones were under threat by time and neglect. Behind were the razed spaces of many others. Only chimneys remained, a minor echo of the famous five chimneys that had come to signify Auschwitz, which in turn came to signify the Holocaust itself. Four of the five had been destroyed: one by rebellion and three by the Germans as the Red Army approached. These smaller chimneys that warmed the barracks remained, though the wooden barracks were gone. The brick stacks seemed especially exposed. They could heat nothing now; they had offered very little heat then, either.

The inside was bare, with three levels of sleeping bunks. It was nearly inconceivable that the space had housed about a thousand, crammed so tightly, seven or eight to a bunk, that all had to turn in bed to accommodate anyone's turn. Volodya excused himself to go to the men's room in the visitor's center. We would meet him near the divide in the tracks.

As we stood in front of the model barracks, taking a moment to get our bearings, we were approached by a stocky middle-aged man, trailed by his reedy adolescent son. The son stood behind his father's shoulder with a blank expression—not quite teenaged resistance but not giving anything away, either.

"Do you know about this place?" the man asked us in a gruff voice, perhaps a Chicago accent. He sounded faintly annoyed.

Despite the tone, I could feel my father relax a little in response. Here was an opportunity to teach, a relief from the obscure tension that had gripped us both on and off for most of the day. For me the dominant feeling was bewilderment, even more intense than what I had felt in Auschwitz I, a sense that I wanted to respond but that the enormity of the ground, the actuality of it, stunned that out of me.

My father began to answer with the head gesture of his that signaled modesty. He wasn't going to claim any expertise. "Well, I do—some things. I nearly was taken here during the war."

"Look at it," the man said, vaguely indicating the surrounding camp with a nod and a small sweep of his hand. "We've been all through it. It's a wreck. Everything's falling down."

I held my tongue. He didn't seem the person with whom to get into the vexed, the philosophical questions of what to do with the camps, of what was appropriate in preservation or restoration.

He went on. "It's the Poles who are in charge of it, right?"

The question seemed mostly rhetorical, but I said yes, sure, it was a

Polish museum now. My father seemed to be waiting for what the man intended to ask that required his knowledge of Auschwitz.

"The Poles don't have the money for it," the man continued. I glanced at my father, our tension restored in a flash, something about the word "money."

And then it came. The son's face over his shoulder still registered nothing as the man delivered exactly what we were wary of, from his sort anyway: "The Jews should take care of this place. They have the money. They could take…"

My father made some sort of sound and took a step toward the man. I didn't know what he was going to do, but feeling the intensity of his anger, I grabbed him around the shoulder and guided his forward momentum quickly past the man. My father, taken by surprise, swung his head around to me, but came along.

"Jason, what…?"

I said to the man as we walked past, "Yeah really, that's what you think? Kind of a German idea."

We went quickly back toward the rails and ramp, to follow the *Lagerstrasse* deeper into the camp. Volodya was heading toward us.

"What were you going to do, yell?" I asked. "Hit the guy?"

"That *bulvan*. That bastard. Here, in this place! What they get with their mother's milk about Jews," my dad sputtered before going silent.

"Nah," I said, "he just doesn't have a clue about what he is saying, and it's complicated. He has come here, after all, and he brought his son, to learn about one of the worst places, the worst things…"

I looked behind us, but that father and son were nowhere in sight. We went slowly through the ramp, trailing several groups of people, two or three in each. But so few visitors. Were others ahead of us? Behind? Were most of the people still lunching, or had all this space, all these acres, diluted a sense of the visiting population? Where was the brisk Israeli couple? No one seemed to linger in the space, conducted onward by the lines of track and road.

I didn't want to stop, either. This was, in some ways, as haunted as the places of execution, a place of separation, the last moments of families as family, where the few spared persons were plucked from the mass of the immediately condemned. Hundreds of thousands on this ground. I could call up the few photographs in my head, the very few images that constituted the sole existing record of that particular horror. Mengele and the other doctors, by turn, separated the living stream, condemning always the vast majority only to different sorts of death, at differing speeds. Today I wondered what the other visitors had in their minds as they passed over the ground, who among the small knots of guideless travelers understood what exactly they were walking on. Very few posted signs to tell: that's the reason for the guides and guidebooks. One would have to know how much more there is than what can be seen, more than can be told. And even then, hearing, being told, allowed for such a minimal understanding. To imagine fully was to court nightmare.

We walked slowly west, toward the gate for the women's camp on the left. The Roma camp lay on our right, directly across from it. A men's camp was next, then another family area, where the people from the "show" camp, Theresienstadt, in Czechoslovakia, had been brought. Farthest east was the quarantine section with reconstructed barracks, large rectangular spaces defined by wire. To the north, bordering all those camps, was Mexiko, a work in progress, meant to greatly extend capacity, adding acreage, almost half again. We were about even with the Theresienstadt camp and my father had dropped back to walk with Volodya. I turned to them.

"*Izvinite*," I said to Volodya," *excuse me*—one of the handful of Russian phrases in my vocabulary. "Dad, the story of Mala and Edek." He gave me a look, a little confused for a moment, and I thought he was going to stop me. But he didn't, and I told him what I knew of the Auschwitz lovers. Edek was Polish, an "old" number, a low number, and younger than Mala. She was a Belgian Jew and spoke several languages. With so many languages in the camp, the Nazis needed interpreters—and runners. So, conditions became more tolerable for her. She was even allowed to grow her hair out. As she circulated on her errands, she grew widely recognized and admired because she used her position to help other prisoners, carrying messages and medicine. He was a mechanic by training, and he had parlayed his abilities into jobs that allowed him, too, movement around the camp.

"These are the lovers, then," he said and then translated for Volodya.

"Yes," I said. "They met somehow and fell in love, managed to keep meeting in secret."

I was certain he would be interested; the motifs of his own survival were present: language, and a mechanic's skills. But we were again in that peculiar position. I would have called this a reversal of roles—he as auditor of a Holocaust account that I gave—except the situation was less and less unusual even before this trip.

"And they escaped from here," I said, "down this very road. Edek wore an SS uniform and she carried a sink, a basin, to hide her face and hair. Out the front gate, an SS escort leading a prisoner on an errand. A little like the way you got out of Csepel in your stolen uniform."

Like and unlike, I supposed. This was Auschwitz, after all. Uniqueness was a given.

I was providing one story from the larger story that he was part of, a story peripheral to his but which might seem to him more central than his own. So while I gave, I also took away. I understood the diminishment he might feel—such a story, set here, one I knew and he didn't, of a suffering greater than his. I had collected many stories at such remove from my own experience that I often felt completely at a loss. But my father's experience, his narratives, forced me to attend to those stories, to try and imagine the suffering, his and others'. Many times I wearied of the effort, and resented it too.

I gave him a chance to pass on a version of what I'd said to Volodya.

"They were free for a week or two before they were retaken," I said, wanting to finish quickly what I had started. We had reached the entrance to the women's camp. "I believe Edek had a chance to get away if he left her—maybe she was stopped by a patrol and he was already up ahead. I forget the details. They were brought back to Block 11 and tortured for days. The SS badly wanted the names of those who had helped get the uniform. Neither gave any names."

I couldn't have said with any precision what proportions of discomfiture and interest I expected for him from the story. I may have been aware of my own ambivalence generally at the time, and my storytelling on this partic-ular occasion surely gathered momentum from it. But the moment wasn't one of awareness. We went through the gate of the women's camp and made for what had been the Hungarian Women's Camp in 1944. I led the way, expecting them to follow and they did. I felt suddenly, absurdly, like a guide. Why absurdly? Because it was my father who had been through it, and Lilly; not me. I was the blind leading the sighted. But what about the actual guides, the people who looked about twenty years younger than me, who had merely studied and been trained? Still, my unease was growing.

Was telling that story insensitive? Especially the part about the brutal interrogations? Yet their names had naturally come up when we were in Block 11 in Auschwitz I, how they had been held in the cells, how Edek had carved their names and numbers on the wall. The desire to tell my father this story was forceful, certainly, but there was no specific source for that desire. What did come to mind later was the fact that my father had been part of many interrogations with the Russians, brutal ones, as he'd indicated but never amplified, hardly ever mentioned. And clearly he had had no choice. Had I reminded him? Had he been reminded? Could he restrict access to those memories?

"Somewhere over there," I said, "that space by those barracks." I pointed vaguely. "I think that's about where they did those hours of roll calls. Near there was where they executed her. Or tried to. Mala had hidden a razor and cut an artery—and struck an SS man when he tried to stop her."

I finished the story. During Mala's struggle she had called out about a coming liberation. The Russians would arrive and the Germans would be made to answer for what they were doing. They carted her off to stop the bleeding and said they were going to put her in the oven alive. Nobody was sure how she died. Edek was hanged back in the men's camp, the next enclosure over by the wooden barracks. He attempted to throw himself at the noose before the SS could put him in it.

Volodya nodded his way through my father's repetition in Russian, looking over at me from time to time, a little quizzically perhaps. It was probably more talk than he had heard out of me during the entire trip.

Throughout the Auschwitz visit, we had separated and rejoined as a matter of course and as the spirit moved us, but now I felt suddenly tired, certainly talked out. I asked my father if he'd mind if I went off on my own. I wanted to find Lilly's barracks and visit the ash ponds and the memorial—all on the western end. We agreed to meet in an hour and a half by the main gate.

Finding Lilly's barracks did not take long, or rather the space it once oc-cupied: a small marker with the number ten, at the corner of a rectangular outline in the grass, nothing more. These buildings had been built of brick salvaged from the village that was disassembled to make way for the camp, and without proper foundations on marshy ground. The structures were intended to be as temporary as the people who inhabited them, a habitation as brief as the Nazis could manage.

The sheer numbers of the Hungarian transports choked everything; the people couldn't be murdered quickly enough. A famous photograph exists of people waiting in the grass among the birches for their turn. For what, none could have had a clear idea, weak and dazed after the torture of the transports, the cruelty of the unloading with the shouting and the blows, everything calculated to keep them disoriented and biddable. Lilly and her sisters had been among them in May 1944. They'd lived here, yards from where I stood; they had paraded naked before Mengele and had been selected again for the munitions plant, which saved them. I waved over at my father and Volodya, gesturing that I was going to the monument. As I went out onto the *Lagerstrasse* again I thought of Lilly and her sisters.

It began, as we had begun our journey, in Munkacs. The Hungarian police had driven the sisters, the whole family, into the ghetto a day af-ter Passover, killing some people to encourage cooperation. Shmuel went; Zlate Raisel went, as did my great-aunt Irene and the seven half-brothers and -sisters of my father. At Seder every year we spoke the words, retold the story of the Exodus—how in every generation we must feel that we ourselves have been redeemed, that we have been brought out of Egypt. The fate of the people is to be felt on the individual level, as is the gratitude for redemption. Birkenau, I thought, as I walked through its pale preserva-tion, was a place better remembered than Egypt, a story told and retold in my lifetime, a story consisting of millions of stories, on this ground and all over Europe. It was modern history, of course, and thus easier to imagine than the ancient sort, which is more like myth than history. But it is thin comfort to take solace in the survival of the people. A people had been redeemed, but "redeemed" seemed altogether the wrong word.

I wandered around, looked at the huge communist-era monument, and the pond of ashes with the inscribed stones before it, commemorating the dead in a number of languages. I made my way over and stood a while near the ruins, the fallen chimney, of crematorium three. As I paced around the area, following a fence line back and forth for a few yards, I could see the "sauna" building. The ruins of Kanada would be between me and it. I believed that was the ground I was looking beyond. Part of the day had been spent in calculations, with a map or the memory of a map, about what we were actually viewing in these near identical spaces, nearly empty, among perhaps a few remnant structures. I understood that the "sauna" had lately opened for visitors. It had been the building where those selected for labor, including Lilly and her sisters, were stripped and herded for the actual showers and delousing. I was not sure I wanted to see the place. I was not sure what else I needed to see, or wanted to.

But just then I did see something, some movement, figures.

It was them, wasn't it, the Israelis? I thought I could make them out, at a distance, in among the birches. She was like a birch herself, tall and pale like those of New England. He was squatter, trunk-heavy, like the trees here. One odd thought followed another: I turned them into a single tree, she, the band of whiteness; he, the dark trunk. But that was a gift of the old gods. The couple in Ovid, for their hospitality, had been melded into trunk and branch, an end-of-life gift for an old couple.

If I were the god of this place, or only that place where they were, walking over ashes, I'd give them another gift, a different sort. I'd have them make a child here, out of their defiance, breaking whatever decorum there could possibly be in this graveyard, the largest in the world. A Jewish child for those Israelis—a different kind of Jew from the Jews who died here. I could just about see them, except I wasn't seeing them. A trick of the mind and eye, I had deputized the Israeli couple to be a vital continuance in this place, against this place, imagining them out there beyond the burning pits and ash dumps, among the birches.

*Shmuel's name on a wall—as Sámuel Steinberger—at the Hungarian state exhibition, Block 18, Auschwitz*

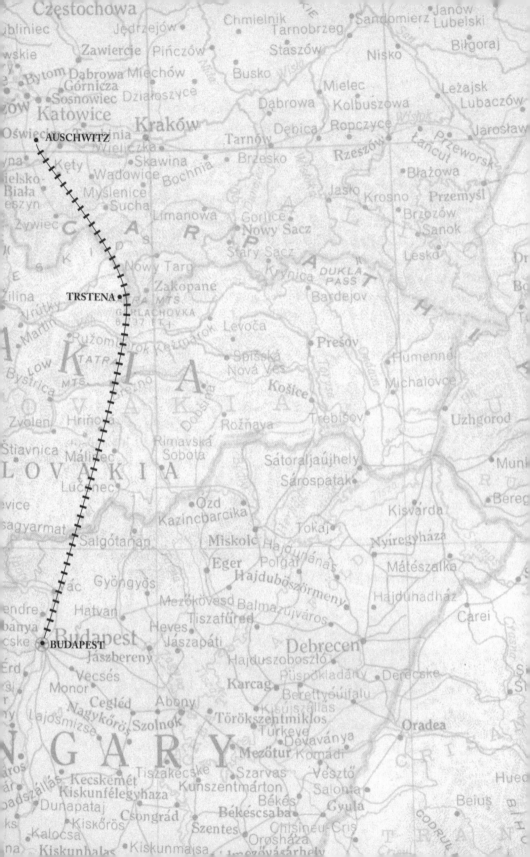

# 11

*To one who knows all languages*
*No human authored sound means nothing*

. . . . . . . . . . . . . . . . . . . . . . . . .

*he hears*
*and overhears, attends and listens*

*to the music of the common*
*origin, past Babel, into Eden.*

AFTER BIRKENAU, what conversation there was in the car, especially between my father and me, was subdued by several kinds of weariness. Even the landscape, a favorite subject for Volodya and my dad, attracted little commentary. The plains around Oswiecim were unremarkable anyhow, and as we began our journey back to Budapest, the final leg of our trip, I looked forward to another view of the Tatra Mountains, if the light held. I wasn't sure how far we had to go and didn't want to bother with the map.

After an hour or so, the Tatras came into view, craggy and imposing. Late afternoon shaded toward evening, and after another hour we approached the Slovak border. Despite the decline of the day, the mood seemed to be lightening among us—a little more chatter as we were about to leave Poland.

The Trstena border control had a hint of service station about it: lanes and a tiny booth with a bigger building off to the side. The service wasn't drive-through, however; Volodya handed our papers through the window and we were waved to the side. The guard told us to get out of the car and then spoke with Volodya. My father stood with me but listened intently. Given his history, he was always tense around borders. Our cheeriness in the car, as we did our best to put Auschwitz behind us, had evaporated— we were now with men in uniform, and there was a faint echo of some kind, ridiculous as that might seem.

The echo got less and less faint for my father as the interaction got more strained. We walked closer to the small booth. I gathered that something was wrong with a visa and that the guard was telling Volodya that he couldn't take himself or his car through Slovakia. Directly behind him, taped against the inside glass of the booth, was a photocopied sheet about visas. Any problems must be handled elsewhere. The guard indicated to Volodya he could make adjustments in Warsaw, a nonsense of both distance and time.

Volodya and my father continued to appeal nonetheless to logic, to ordinary human consideration. I didn't need to understand most of the words to recognize that the tones were the tones of reason. I could see the young guard would not—could not—respond to this; a man in his late twenties or early thirties, he was only following orders. That catchphrase, the German perpetrator's excuse, did come to mind. He shrugged, pointed to the posted sign, and crisply repeated, "Warsaw." While I thought it was East-European absurd for a man from the Ukraine not to be allowed to cross a neighboring border, something in me accepted the terms immediately. I was sure anyway the fellow (and his portly supervisor, who had been summoned) wouldn't relent. I recognized the presence of greater political forces dwarfing a particular case, a harmless situation that should have required exception.

Volodya would have to return to Ukraine through Poland—and then on to Hungary with us, though that made no sense. It was three times the distance, and besides, our single-entry Ukrainian visa precluded returning. Volodya's ordinarily forceful tones had risen to the verge of anger, and the border guard's stance made clear that any more argument would be not only useless but dangerous. He ushered Volodya to the car to see him off. Another guard followed and I came along to get our bags. I watched him disappear down the road, the sun low in the sky.

Volodya was reft from us. It felt no less than that, especially after the intensity of the last few days. His removal felt ominous. Not merely his expulsion, but the realization, not fully formed at that point, that he had been the person who had insured our expedition—and in more ways than were immediately obvious. As I saw him drive away, I wondered again at the extent of his knowledge. Of rivers, of people—perhaps more than he indicated about railways and bridges, too. He had underwritten us psychologically as well, stepping closer and stepping away at the right moments. The extent to which that quality—his instinctual tact—mattered was coming to me then and there, marooned in a definitional nowhere between one country and another. My father and I were sole journeyers again, as we had been in the beginning. Yet I was calm. This borderland seemed to suit me precisely somehow for the moment—the apt location for my version of diaspora, in suspension, neither one place nor another in my thinking or my person. If I had started to prod at a few things I didn't expect a conclusion. I had destinations but no way to get there yet.

I headed back to the booth with our two rolling cases and saw that my dad did not share my calm. We were in uncertain circumstances but no danger, yet he was registering our uncertainty with absolute panic. He seemed to shrink—trembling, transformed into a frail version of his age. His recourse was pleading, the tones unmistakable, close to tears, trailing our original guard, he said, in Czech now, "I am a Holocaust survivor." I had heard him say that calmly in a number of languages—in a self-deprecating way—but here he begged nakedly. As if this time a plea might matter to men in uniform. In the midst of the Slavic babble that phrase appeared over and over again.

My first response was intense embarrassment and then, unaccountably, laughter. I choked it back and ran for him. I faced him, put my hands on his shoulders, and tried to make him focus on me, but his eyes swung everywhere.

"Dad, Dad, it's all right. It's all right."

The guard finally turned toward us. "Taxi" was the one word I could make out. He wasn't suggesting a taxi to Budapest, was he? No, he must have meant into Trstena, where we could make other arrangements. And without offering us use of a phone, he walked off to meet a tour bus that had pulled into the station.

"Dad, what's the matter? We'll get back." He was still looking around, a little wild-eyed, not yet himself. "Dad, can I do something? Can I get you some water? What can I do?"

The last question voiced a fear that had whispered to me from the start—that I wouldn't be able to do something; that for comfort I would be unreliable or inept, lacking in ability and, at some crucial moment, maybe even desire.

My dad's relationship with borders had to do with history. They had shifted frequently when he was a boy, crossing him without him crossing them, advancing misery for Jews. Later, he would cross them—or attempt to—at times when the effort often meant life or death. At a border his chief nightmare was not disorder—he had made it through many chaotic borders, with help, out of Hungary and Czechoslovakia and from Austria over the Alps to Italy. No, his true nightmare was the opposite, *order*, the implacable arrangement of guards and their rules, the men in uniform following orders and arrayed against him.

What so terrified him, it seemed to me, was a profound disordering made to appear ordered, made into law, full of irrational, codified jeopardy, a penalty for simply being. The anti-Jewish laws of Hungary and Germany went beyond the Kafkaesque terrors of being on trial for an unknown offense or waking up as an insect. My father had been merely another roach among the millions of designated roaches, charged with, guilty of Jew.

Yet how could I know whether it was one thing or the other—total breakdown or evil lockstep or something else entirely? After all, my father was an omnivore of terror; he had suffered the most thorough dissolutions of social order: in the midst of war, at the edges of war, behind enemy lines; on foot in his own country and on horseback in the army of another. He'd had law and border shift around him, restricting his life, collecting him for forced labor, while narrowly avoiding what he feared most, the fate of almost all his family.

So I imagined my understanding, again, as an arrival at some possible fixed point, when what I ought to have understood was its fluidity. Proof of that arrived with the return of our border guard. He hadn't been gone for more than a few minutes, and his disengaged manner was still entirely intact. However, he had approached a tour bus stopping next in Budapest to ask whether they would be willing to take us. The bus carried a group of Korean dentists ultimately headed for Austria. My father, still shaky, spoke in English to the Russian woman who led the tour. She had a kind of professional friendliness that switched on and off in an instant. And flickered a little with us. She appeared initially dubious and asked to see our passports. My father told her he was a Holocaust survivor but what seemed to interest her—though perhaps she had registered what he said—was that he was traveling with his son. She said she must check with the bus group and disappeared to do so. They agreed, but the Slovak driver saw an opportunity and wanted two hundred dollars for the trip. Dad is a born bargainer—and the man's attempt at profiteering was restorative. More emotional appeals followed from Dad, but with a dash of canniness now, in Czech, "I am not a millionaire; I am a schoolteacher." The driver reluctantly agreed to a fifty-dollar reduction.

When the guide asked how she should introduce us to the dentists and their spouses, my father became a professor again. We stood at the front of the bus and they applauded us in, bowing as we moved to our seats. We bowed in return, and several of them came back and presented us with business cards, with more bowing. Every now and then one or another of the dentists near us would lean out into the aisle and nod a bow and we would return bow for bow. But none even attempted conversation—in English or anything else.

I allowed myself a little schadenfreude at this turn of events. The polyglot's languages were suddenly neutralized. We were surrounded by Korean in this luxury liner of a bus, moving through the hills of Slovakia, and Dad could have the rare experience—a commonplace for me on this trip—of utter linguistic incomprehension. He began to settle into calm by degrees. But I was troubled too.

A few hours earlier, when we were approaching the Slovak border with Volodya, I had begun to look forward to this part of the journey. The task we had set ourselves had been completed as successfully as we were able. We were free now to explore other matters, other places; Dad could show me where he had been and tell me what he thought of where he had been—then, later, now. He could be the unalloyed focus of the rest of our journey. From time to time, I sensed in him the constraints that I felt partly responsible for. We had certainly visited places of great importance to him already, those he had shared with Shmuel in Munkacs and those he hadn't in Budapest. Still, I believed he had held himself back, as near as I could tell, given the unpredictable way he allowed himself to remember or resist memories. I thought of Oktogon Square and his passing through without comment.

Yet alongside my sense of accomplishment, I felt a little cheated. We were going through, going past, other sites in my father's story, areas he had traversed with his Red Army unit in Slovakia. Had we still been with Volodya, we would have had the freedom to go explore, if inclined, and perhaps put other of my father's ghosts to rest—and do for me whatever it was that I still seemed to need. It was as if once started with this level of involvement in his story, I found this sudden stopping short difficult. After our bridge, after our visit to Auschwitz, after these days of travel, I still had the impulse to continue, still felt there was more to do to clear the path between us. And I believed that there might be more chances to do that. But a side trip to Jolsva, his first labor camp and the start of his friendship with Imre, was now out of the question. There was more to say about Imre, I was certain. I had more to ask, anyway.

As the evening deepened, my father and I sat side by side, looking out the bus's large windows at the landscape, hilly and lovely in the twilight. A castle on a hill seemed to grow out of it in the most precise way, the walls continuous with the slopes that led up to them, as if the rock and greenery of the hillside had simply organically transformed into cut stone blocks. My father seemed at peace after his terrible panic at the border. Here we were and, with the exception of the chilly tour guide, well to the front, I was the only person he could speak to. But we didn't speak much. I needed no map; the road signs we passed had towns whose names I'd heard from him, Slovakian towns his Red Army unit had passed through.

"Dad, there is the story you used to tell, a good one—one of my favorites, anyway—and you used to tell it well, I thought."

He looked from the window to me, expectantly.

"About the time you captured, sort of, this group of Germans—not so far from here, I think?"

Using a motorcycle the Russians had taken from the Germans, my dad had been on an errand and was headed back to his outpost when the accelerator cable broke and the bike coasted to a halt. Dismounting, he began to wheel the machine back. Around him in the bright day lay forest and field and country stillness, not even distant sounds of fighting—no crackle of small-arms fire or thud of bombardment. He would emphasize the quiet because of how loud the sudden rustling was when a group of soldiers emerged from the trees: five Germans, with their rifles trained on him. He was certain he was going to die and just stood there, gripping the handlebars.

*A reminder of his motorcycling days with the Russians: Dad in Cremona posing on a Jawa like the one he used during his time in the Red Army*

They seemed nervous; a few kept looking up and down the road, while one asked if my dad was *allein* or were there *andere*, others, more Russian soldiers following him? He answered in German, taking in how worn the group appeared, dirty with ragged uniforms, only a couple with helmets. He was alone, he said, on his way back to headquarters in the next village. He saw that his German, rudimentary as it was, eased their tension. He hoped they wouldn't consider his uniform too carefully or why he spoke German; his lack of visible insignia of rank, along with the epaulets, was a mark of the intelligence services. Their spokesman explained that they wanted to surrender and my father understood immediately. Their army was in retreat in Slovakia, and this group had been cut off. The Germans sought a measure of safety by surrendering to a numerically inferior enemy, believing it minimized the possibility of immediate mistreatment.

Dad collected their weapons, slung and cradled, and followed behind as the Germans pushed the motorcycle, three or four at a time, one or two rotating out and walking beside. Progress into the village was slow, and as they got closer, my father unholstered his pistol and made an effort to appear to be "covering" his prisoners. By the time they reached the building requisitioned for the unit's use, there were perhaps ten soldiers out front, with the captain, in a mock ceremonial gauntlet for the hero's welcome. They held paper cutouts of medals—the order of Lenin—with pins and tacks. The Germans were roughly carted off, and my father was whirled through the crowd and roughly pinned to the flesh with the medals, pounded on the back, and feted with congratulatory expressions, most of which addressed him as "little Jew."

When I first heard him tell of this experience, I focused on the adventure—my father in the war, with a motorcycle and guns. I came to appreciate his humiliation, not just at the finale but throughout his experience in that army, as well as the outright danger. Neither shame nor risk became the dominant note in his narration. The incident was another close call, another reprieve; a variation on the theme of luck, with a hint of providence in the background. But then he stopped telling the story. He hadn't fallen generally silent, and plenty of opportunities presented themselves, but the anecdote disappeared. As I learned more about that war, more about the Red Army, more about my father, I thought I understood his silence. But now we were close to where it happened, and it seemed right to ask him about it.

"You know, where you came back with the prisoners and they hazed you, with paper orders of Lenin? Well, practically kicked the crap out of you."

"Yes, they knew what had happened. By the way, it happened then at the end of the war to other soldiers there."

"Perhaps not the full ceremony, the full treatment—for the Jew."

"No, maybe not."

"But, Dad, you haven't mentioned the capture thing for years, and I..."

"Really, I just didn't have it in my mind..."

"It's because of the prisoners, isn't it? Because of what the Russians did to them."

My father didn't answer for a moment, only looked at me, his face slackening into weariness, then he nodded slowly several times and turned to the window. "I am going to close my eyes for a little."

Around us, curtains were being drawn and the bus's video screens came alive with the opening credits of the *Sound of Music*, subtitled in Korean, and then Julie Andrews in the Alps, spinning toward the circling camera: the group's preparation for the Austrian section of their tour.

I let him be a while, as I watched the landscape descend into utter darkness, relieved at intervals by the lights of towns. He wouldn't sleep long in these conditions, if he slept at all. Would I broach other subjects that this landscape would bring to mind? I did very much want to—some sense of possibility was in the night, the quiet, the weariness, our being isolates together—after having shared so much experience. All of that mattered somehow, suggested I should try to overcome his reluctance. But would it overcome mine?

He rarely spoke of his involvement with prisoners. His job, after all, had been to translate during interrogations. Beyond a few specific references to the Russians' fierce shouting at captives, he was vague about cruelties he had witnessed. The translation stories I recall him telling—during one period especially—concerned his role as a go-between for Smirnov with women, rendering the Russian's proffers. One scene he described, for comic effect, took place on a couch in a commandeered home—my father literally in the middle, between Smirnov and a woman, passing along the increasingly specific seductions until Dad was dismissed and the couple adjourned to the bedroom. Smirnov was pure id but with a gun and a unit of soldiers. He had the power of life and death as well as access to looted bounty—and food. Dad had often mentioned his hatred for the brutality of the entire experience, the drunkenness and Jew-baiting within the ranks and the regular violence of the troops toward civilians. The rapes were what most shocked and disgusted him. He couldn't speak of them beyond expressing abhorrence. He had been an innocent with an absolute reverence for women that came from being raised by the one who was his hero. But I was curious about what further thoughts he might have had about being part of, albeit unwillingly, Captain Smirnov's sort of courtship.

Perhaps another episode provided a clue: the couch narrative had a related anecdote prior to his stint with Smirnov and the Red Army, centering on an awful chance he took once; twice, really. Newly liberated by the Russians, he had arrived in Budapest on foot, happening on the Oktogon Square executions. Sporadic fighting continued even on the Pest side, and the Germans still held Buda. A man of military age would have had every reason to avoid notice of any kind. But commotion in an open courtyard caught his attention as he wandered past: a drunken soldier had cornered a young woman, and her family was begging him to let her go. Almost before he knew it, Dad had roared in Russian for him to leave her alone. To his surprise the soldier lurched away. The reward for the rescue was shelter for the night, which came with yet another opportunity for rescue. A pair of Russian soldiers forced their way into the apartment in the middle of the night looking for more to drink and whatever else of value they could find. As the intruders began taking an interest in the daughter, Dad pretended to be the young woman's husband, saving her again. He spoke of his initial intervention as an impulse he hardly knew he followed. The second he minimized as merely going along with the suggestion of the girl's father.

The confrontations seemed particularly brave, but I wondered whether there was anything of mitigation in his recounting, however modestly presented. He seemed unaware of how the other story could sound, a sort of pandering. I wondered if he connected the two incidents; that the earlier demonstrations of courage on behalf of women were offered as a balance to the latter activities with Smirnov. I wondered also at the condition of his own consciousness. A complex understanding of events as they had unfolded—in the labor camps, on the run, in the army—constituted a luxury he could not afford back then, in the midst. He was trying to survive, but afterward—what did he think now of then? Did he second-guess, even first-guess, his choices? Or did necessity come with a built-in pardon, and a pass on reconsideration? If I knew that, I would know something significant about him. What did it mean that I didn't?

I looked over at him, his head rolling side to side, nodding down and jerking up. He couldn't be comfortable. I re-draped his jacket around him. At the same time, I had a flash of an old resentment: here I was again, trying to puzzle him out—but did he ever think of me in that way? Did he ever think about what I was thinking, in a way specific to me, to who I was? The all-purpose nostrums for everyone—to banish Holocaust from our hearts by applying love, as he recommended to that high school audience—could he have thought that would strike me as profound, "play" for me at all?

I tried not to rouse Dad at the border check as we crossed between Slovakia and Hungary, getting his passport from his bag, but we had some trouble on the Hungarian side. After getting our passports back from the Slovaks, apparently the driver neglected to stop for the Hungarian officials. We were alerted to this oversight when the police chased us down and the long bus was compelled to maneuver a fragmented U-turn on the two-lane road. Escorted back to the border, we all handed in our passports and waited and waited and waited as the Hungarians reasserted their authority, and then some.

The driver, though quick to seize an opportunity to gouge us, was not terribly bright; both his Russian and English, useful in the region, were minimal, his Hungarian nonexistent. Dad volunteered his aid and smoothed things over with the guards, who eventually returned our passports. One of the dentists helped with distribution, moving through the bus, opening them and handing them out. At first, he gave me the driver's, who bore little resemblance to me aside from our beards. I considered what mischief I might perform as I held on to it and then retrieved my own, but I didn't want to cause problems for our kind Korean hosts, so I passed it on to the driver. Besides, my dad was on the phone to the hotel explaining we would be in late. The driver had been compelled to ask him for help, and I could tell my father was pleased. It was his version of not only getting even

171

but pulling ahead. His languages and his usefulness showed up the driver, restored in Dad a sense of superiority, and, more importantly, demonstrated it to others. That was all the comeuppance he required.

Dad's friendliness, charm, and emotional appeals had not impressed initially, but in the end they did. It struck me how I recognized, even identified with the sense of security provided by winning the regard of strangers. They—others, strangers, gentiles (was this a Jew thing?)—might have remained indifferent, and if they had any power over us, their casual approval would be especially precious, a measure of their initial indifference or even contempt. The familiarity of the calculus didn't lie merely in recognizing Dad's concerns in the interaction, with the driver and the others around us. I realized I had often done versions of that myself, clowning for the tough kids in the Bronx, and later on in dicey moments of solo travel in the Middle East. Maybe anyone would try to be admired or to please—for self-preservation, simply a natural human behavior. How frequently it was practiced depended on how much, and how often, one felt under threat. Still, it could well have been something I had gotten from him.

As we set out on the short ride from the border to Budapest, I began thinking of Dad's time in labor camps. We had passed fairly close to Jolsva, and with any possibility of a visit lost, the place-name had become an emblem of what more could be said that might not be. We would also pass not far from the airfield where he'd labored after Jolsva and before Csepel. To Jolsva he'd been brought by train—yes, cattle cars and straw, but nothing like the transports, Dad said often—not to be compared to them, not so bad as the trains to the death camps. As a child I had been bewildered by that insistence, and it later drove me crazy. "Wasn't so bad" for him was not so good for me. I had some stake in it being bad enough. If it weren't, why his nightmares, why the stories, why had so much in our lives revolved around that monumental *thing* that he had been caught up in? How bad did something have to be to be considered on its own terms, to qualify without comparison to anything else? Was all that misery second-class misery? What I'd heard from him, though, were experiences I couldn't imagine living through; so much of what happened to him seemed too much for me. I couldn't have stood it. I would have died.

On the grounds of suffering alone, I understood myself to be the lesser person, so much further from the flames than my father. Wasn't I meant to understand myself as less? Jewishness seemed to me to be as much about withstanding and learning from suffering as other accomplishments. Without that endurance, the values of Jewishness—that ark of arks, ark that carries a remnant through the flood, ark that keeps the covenant, ark that houses the Torah in every synagogue in the world—would have vanished. Though my relationship with the Torah was uncertain—I considered it more a trove of stories than the font of law—I knew it was at the center. In and around it, attached to it, was a culture with manifold expressions of humane understanding, critical assessment, mystical immanence. The ethical freight at the heart, though, was "Love thy neighbor as thyself," or as Rabbi Hillel famously put it in response to a gentile's goading request to sum up the entire Bible standing on one foot, "What is hateful to you do not do to your neighbor. The rest is commentary." He added. "Now go and study." All those cultural goods faced with so much evil and rendered more precious for being under threat of annihilation; all of it carried by people, *a* people, that so many others for so long wanted extinguished.

Nearly everything in my life gave me to know the terrible preciousness of those who had escaped to tell, to carry on with Judaism and Jewishness. Clearly, those who suffered and managed to salvage their lives, their Jewish lives, would be of the highest value. And those were the survivors and that was not me. I was proof of life's continuance. The children of survivors had to understand themselves as versions of Job's rewards. We might make ourselves worthy if we embraced and transmitted, teaching diligently to our children what Jewishness had given us.

Dad was surfacing now from sleep, rubbing his hands over his face. I was still thinking of Jolsva, which had been the beginning of what was intended to be the end for my father, though not as bad as any term in a death camp, where most of his group were murdered. If Auschwitz was hell's core, Jolsva and Csepel were outer circles, which he had shared with Imre.

We planned on visiting Csepel while in Budapest, before heading back to the US. My mind turned to an additional character from that camp, a different hero, a man my father had asked me to record in a poem. A few years before this trip, I had been visiting my parents in New York. I was getting ready to leave, and my mother was in the kitchen packing too much fruit for my return flight to St. Louis. Dad called me into his study, where he sat behind the lagoon-shaped teak desk, Danish modern, the purchase guided by my mother, no doubt. Lists of words lay in front of him as always and several books, including a hefty dictionary for boning up on one of his languages, typically making use of every minute while I packed. Hungarian that day, I saw. He asked me to sit across from him and, though I was about to plead the rush of departure, something in his voice, a deliberateness, a formality, prompted me to sit. Over his shoulder, I could see one of my books ceremonially positioned with keepsakes—a matryoshka, a plaque—on a shelf. I have often wondered, often doubted, whether he read my books. A talk seemed to be on the way, or information he had that I should have: the location of important papers…if anything happens… your mother is going in for a procedure, nothing serious, a women's matter. It turned out to be a different topic altogether.

"You know about Gunga Din, the man we called that in Csepel? He carried water for us at forced labor?"

I knew he hadn't meant the literary character, but the man from the camp.

He went on: "You write sometimes from stories I have told you. Will you write about him? A poem?"

Perhaps glancing at my poems or reviewing Hungarian had prompted this commission, this charge. I should do something to honor the man they'd nicknamed Gunga Din for his service as a water carrier to the Jews at slave labor. With others, my father had hoisted scrap into the maw of the factory's smelter: broken rails, locomotive wheels, engine casings thrown into a cauldron of fire, a circle of heat almost unbearable. It was like a scene from Dante, though I'd heard the story many times before I even knew who Dante was.

I heard the first telling as an eleven-year-old, when I accompanied my parents to a grown-up dinner at a lawyer's house—a house so big, our entire one-bedroom apartment would have fit into its minimalist, open-plan first floor with its white walls and paintings. I was its incidental audience, hearing it at a distance as I sat on a sofa with a book, at the audible border but listening hard. Dad knew better than to speak to me directly then anyway; I was a seething fumarole of resentments, iced over in irony when I could muster it. I counted on him missing my faint sarcasm, a ploy dangerous with a European father who was as heavy-handed as any on our block, these men with accents who shouted from windows or stoops and were apt to descend to the street and smack their kids around for various reasons.

My father sometimes lost himself entirely to anger. It felt as though anything could happen to someone caught in the midst, someone who caused, and therefore deserved, the anger. Something must have been deeply wrong with a child who required such force in response. But it wasn't the episodes of anger alone that fueled resentment. After all his absences for so many night-school nights came his starring presences, as on that visit—his stories, only *his* story in our closed narrative economy, all the space for story taken up as he recounted his narrow passage to survival with the charm that I thought of as deception, believing I had seen his truest face in rage.

He'd been lucky, that's all, he said to the two other couples there. He waggled his head as he said this, signifying a modesty that suddenly looked out of place, a familiar gesture of his that seemed properly to belong to the countrymen of Gunga Din, though not the one he was talking about. So, when he spoke on that evening to those people about his virtuous Gunga Din, I looked for what he meant in other than what he said, the early stages of the habit. Part of his luck was knowing Gunga Din, to whom he remained ever grateful, the water carrier who never rested, never walked, ran always, bringing water to those my father called brothers. Gunga Din only ever paused to wait as they fed the smelter, standing by as they lifted together great rafts of steel checker plate, large sections of discarded machinery, heavy weights of metal, into the molten roiling. Anyone's momentary slackening, anyone's stumble, might mean a deadfall of iron on everyone. And Gunga Din was at hand always, offering the filled ladle to each, tenderly, as if it were, in my father's description, a meal he had especially prepared for each. I visualized a tiny man, always in a stooped scurry, hunched over, yoked like an ox, buckets hung on either side, ferrying from the pump into the hot exhalations of the hell's mouth smelter and back again.

I heard the story many times over the years. And I came to see Gunga Din as someone who allowed himself to be an incidental figure in someone else's story. Other to the others. Likely even a simpleton, given his frantic motion, even in his service. A water boy in the company of men. They had the harder work, no matter how hard he'd made his own; they formed the brotherhood under the pressure of the most difficult and dangerous job. He must have stood outside of the group, the boy beside those more manly, those who were closer to the fire.

When my dad asked me, that day in New York, to write a poem, I wanted to ask about the nickname. How close a comparison to the hero of Kipling's poem did the men who gave the name intend? I had seen, as they must have, the silly 1939 film inflated out of the poem. The homely, pockmarked Jew Sam Jaffe (his surname means "pretty" in Hebrew) played some kind of approximate Indian. Was he a Sikh in that turban? Of course, Jews often played the other, including Native Americans, cavalry fodder in Westerns. No doubt many Jewish actors were in the verminous swarm of attackers that hurled themselves at the fort the British heroes defended. Their faces were other and being other, they could be any kind of other. So wasn't this man other to them, the Jews at the smelter? They could give him a name besides his own.

"What was his real name?" I asked my father.

He hesitated a little. "I don't know."

"You forgot?"

"We always called him Gunga Din."

"What language did you speak with him?"

I thought maybe they spoke Yiddish, *mamaloshen*, mother tongue.

"Oh, Hungarian."

"And did you talk to him much?"

My father seemed a little distant for a moment. "He had a family, a wife, children."

"The nickname must have been a sort of joke. They laughed at him, right?"

"No, no, no," my father said, drawing himself up and back in his chair, looking at me with surprise. "We loved him."

And in that moment that I believed him, I saw what he meant for me to see: a whole world beyond irony, full of unintricate acts, and love there as simple as slaked thirst.

I told him I would try to write the poem.

And I had tried, though not yet completed it. Now, on the bus to Budapest, I felt I was the one who had to press *him* about Gunga Din, to ask him did he remember, to urge him to take me to the place they had been together. We had to honor him too, didn't we? My father would respond to that. I could truthfully say, too, it might help me finish the poem in the man's memory.

"You know how you once asked me to write about a man in Csepel with you, the guy who hauled water?"

"Yes? Oh, yes, Gunga Din."

"I have been working on a poem about him, but I'd like to see the place. I thought we would have gone."

"Sure. Sure. Tomorrow, we will go to Csepel."

"You were going to take us there, right?"

"Of course, did you think we weren't?"

"I didn't know. We had mentioned when we first arrived and then somehow we did other things. Now we only have a couple of days."

"It was only the time—two trams, at least, or else the train. Would have been easy with Volodya. And I expected he would be with us."

"So, tomorrow morning."

"When we get up, first thing. But maybe not early. It's so late now."

"Fine, Dad. Whenever we can get there."

# 12

*addressing those who've had the privilege*
*of afterwards and elsewhere, luxurious*
*Americans, children even when they're grown.*
*These children, theirs or others, ask their stories,*
*attracted to extremity as to*
*a laboratory of the true....*

AS IT TURNED OUT, we visited a number of places before Csepel. After the long night on the bus, the next day we stayed close to our apartment, returning several times so Dad could rest. I napped too. We ate dinner at Eva's, and Dad filled her in on the days since Uzhhorod. I didn't push Dad about Csepel. I had his promise and trusted he would keep it. Much of this end part of our trip would seem out of order, anyway, compared to the quest for the bridge—the simplicity of the route as originally conceived: Munkacs to Auschwitz, led by the train tracks. Even the return from Auschwitz, which should have included some meandering through places relevant to my father's experience, had been forced into a direct line back to Budapest. Now it was almost as if we accepted a random drift to various locations, in and out of the overlapping histories they entailed, from those personal to Dad to those that represented the larger surround—war and the general fate of Hungarian Jews. There may have been an assortment of places, but the grim themes of our whole trip persisted in them.

A twenty-minute walk from the apartment brought us to the huge

Gothic revival parliament building on the Danube, lit beautifully at night. My appreciation of its aesthetics was troubled by consciousness of all the anti-Jewish laws that had been passed there, starting well before the war. On the banks of this lovely river, somewhere near here, Arrow Cross thugs, Hungarian fascists, had massacred thousands of Jews. I had never heard the phrase "shot into" before I read that history—how Jews and other undesirables had been forced to take off their shoes and were "shot into" the river.

We also visited Buda Castle with Eva, our one foray to the Buda side of the Danube. An elderly passerby, an amateur historian, gave us an account in fluent English of the end of the Siege of Budapest, describing the weeks of fierce German and Hungarian resistance in this stronghold. He talked a lot of the massive civilian casualties among the Hungarians during the siege, the brutalization after. The castle and the city around it had been all but leveled. Did he guess we were Jews, tracking our own losses? Did that show somehow, or was it crazy of me even to have in mind? Dad seemed preoccupied, uncharacteristically contributing little, translating intermittently for Eva, who was aware of the history anyway.

Eva returned to work and Dad and I had lunch in a small café. We made our way back to the apartment, where I picked up the video camera. I had recorded little since Auschwitz. Now it had seemed less necessary, almost an aftermath. We passed the opera, another one of the many handsome nineteenth-century structures that had made the city the "jewel on the Danube." Jews were an important part of its history: Mahler had been music director and many others had performed there until laws restricted and then excluded them.

We visited the Jewish quarter, consciously seeking out some frank commemoration of Jewish presence. The Dohány Street Synagogue, built in the 1850s, had stood at the border of the main ghetto in 1944. Now restored to its full Moorish revival magnificence, it was unique in many ways beyond its striking onion domes and octagonal towers—the biggest synagogue in Europe, second biggest in the world, and the only one permitted to house the dead, a temporary burial at liberation made permanent. Over two thousand lay in its grounds, some of the casualties of the ghetto—dead by starvation and exposure chiefly. We wandered the huge interior, gazing up at the wonderful geometric ceiling decorations.

During my awestruck moments, Dad had gotten into conversation with a group of middle-aged women. Something about his gestures suggested he was talking about himself—the modesty head waggle. I was happy to see him a bit more animated than he had been. At the same time, I thought of my mother's frequent complaint—how other people were always more interesting to him than we were. She often wanted more of his attention; I often wanted less. After a while I swung by to collect him. We made a brief stop at the small museum. Among the inevitable, if beautiful, ritual objects—Torah pointers to help read the text, and jewelry, breastplates, and crowns for "dressing" the scrolls. There was a remarkable Roman-era Jewish grave marker. The figures of a man, woman, and child were incised on it. Was that an indication of a domestic tragedy? Nearby in the Holocaust section we came on a display case of interesting desecrations—a frock made out of prayer shawls, and the vellum pages of a Torah scroll repurposed as drumheads.

"Dad, what do you feel like when you see all this stuff? Not only drums out of Torahs…"

"Well, it's sad, no? What do you mean?"

"I don't know. Even I—and nobody was trying to kill me—even I feel like a returning ghost."

"Oh, Jason."

"No, look—these bits and pieces seem like what is left. You take away the people and have objects that they used, an exhibit for a museum."

"The synagogue is still in use. There are still Jews here."

We strolled out behind the synagogue to Raoul Wallenberg Memorial Park, named for the man who saved thousands of Jews by distributing false Swedish papers. I called Dad over to the brass sign.

"Look," I said and pointed.

*May this park commemorate as an exclamation mark for post-Holocaust generations the name of the Swedish diplomat.*

"Yes, what's the matter?"

"As an 'exclamation mark.' A really peculiar expression, no?"

"I suppose it is."

And I continued reading aloud: "*May it also remind all of the hundreds of thousands of Jewish martyrs, of the labour-camp inmates who died unknown, and of all those righteous who putting their own lives at risk, saved persecutees of certain death.*"

"The park should remind 'all' of 'all'—all of us should be reminded of all the righteous," I said.

"It's the 'alls,' the words?"

"Yes, sure, the words, and the 'righteous'—foreign diplomats *all*, by the way—saved 'persecutees *of* certain death.' 'Of' instead of 'from.' And 'persecutees'?"

"So the English is not so good. They didn't get poets."

"But why, why wouldn't they—whoever—take some care, more care, if they were going to have English?"

He was looking at me and glanced around, perhaps concerned we'd be overheard. Or that I would be. "But look at the sculpture; isn't it beautiful?"

We turned fully toward it—the silvery weeping willow tree with names on every leaf. It seemed to teem and tremble with light of the afternoon.

"Isn't that care?"

"Yes, Dad, it is—a kind of precision of care, in its way—that I'd want the words to have, too."

"Well, we can go, maybe."

The next day, our last full day in Budapest, we headed finally for Csepel, passing again through Oktogon Square for the tram. My father had yet to mention the executions he'd seen here—the hangings from the lampposts. And I had waited for that memory to be revived in him, but if it had been, he never mentioned it. So I finally did.

"Wasn't this the place, the Oktogon, when you were liberated by the Russians and returned, where you saw the hangings?"

He stopped a moment, looked around, and pointed in the direction we'd come. "Yes, it was here, over that way, I think."

"Did you think about it as we came through before?"

"I knew where I was, of course."

"You wrote me once about it. Anyway, I did some research. It wasn't quite what you thought, not spontaneous, a lynching, and it wasn't the Russians who did. It was Hungarians, a provisional government and not just communists. I guess they were empowered by the Russians. The two men had been tried and condemned by the People's Tribunal."

"But they killed those men and there was a crowd watching, cheering some of them. Ugly."

"Yes, but those men, Rotyis—I can't remember the other's name—they were responsible for the murder of over a hundred Jews, forced laborers like you. Would you have felt differently if you knew that?

"I don't know, Jase. I had already seen plenty die and this just made me sick, whatever was the reason for killing them that way."

I thought of one of the most famous pictures of the Vietnam War—a man in a short-sleeved shirt being summarily executed in the street by a uniformed soldier with a pistol shot to the head. Legally, as it turned out. The victim was an infiltrator who had been killing his executioner's comrades moments before, including a general and his family, reportedly. The laws of war permitted the act. But my reaction, along with that of thousands, even after understanding the circumstances, was still revulsion.

"You know, Dad, people were angry at the Jews later because of the hangings. Didn't seem quite right to many Hungarians that the executions were because of what happened to Jews."

"Hey, I think that's our tram coming. We better hurry."

After Jolsva, and an interlude working on an airfield near Budapest, my father arrived in Csepel in May 1944, part of a forced-labor battalion

*An entrance to an underground bunker in the Csepel works, where forced laborers slept, exposed to frequent heavy bombardment*

of about three hundred men. They joined other workers (forty thousand at the height of the war) at the Manfred Weiss Steel and Metalworks on Csepel Island, which also held other Jewish internees who would be taken from there to death camps. The island ghetto was one of many formed around the country soon after the German takeover of Hungary—done to prevent its pullout of the losing Axis cause—to facilitate selection for the transports. Throughout that summer the deportations to Auschwitz continued, but my dad avoided the transports by his luck but also by his labor, once his skill at welding had been discovered.

The majority of the working population left each evening, and slave laborers who were enterprising enough to adjust their dress and organize a worker's identity badge might join them, if they had the good fortune not to be recognized. In mid-August, my dad and his friend Imre Naiman carefully removed the yellow stripes from their sleeves, doctored the newly revealed gap so it blended with the rest, took up their stolen worker's identity cards, and walked out of those gates never to pass through them again. Had they been caught it would have been a noose or a bullet for both. Dad had been forced to witness executions, including the hanging of a friend. He would see the place only once more, long after the war, when my parents stopped there on their way to Munkacs in 1991.

But that earlier visit was not a visit: the factory was utterly deserted back then, he'd told me, though I'd discovered in my research that parts of the complex had been functional. The communist-era protocol of not admitting visitors was no doubt still strong in the early nineties, though I also had the impression that Dad hadn't tried very hard to get in. But now, as we headed to the island together, Hungary was a decade out of the Soviet grasp, and Csepel was open.

I wondered what my father's expectations were, though I didn't ask. These were his subjects to raise in the same way the itinerary was his. The etiquette around survivors had felt particularly binding on this trip, and by and large I had kept it. With my mother, he had posed by the front gate, his escape gate, and walked part of the walled-off periphery, before leaving. The merest form of a visit. Today promised more substance, and I was pleased at that, eager to avoid a kind of ceremonial base-touching around the settings of his stories. I had prepared, as well, to frame his experience with some history.

I don't think it occurred to me that having more to see might be painful to him. And I did not see my silence as an attempt to maintain an element of surprise. On the other hand, I felt more than once that his personal history flowed through a too-well-regulated channel. And my response to such feelings was often shame. If I didn't doubt the facts of his story, how could I doubt the telling? What exactly was I doubting? But whatever I had felt at the time, I looked forward to being present for his response to the place after an absence of nearly sixty years—for the genuineness of a first revival of memory.

Of course, there might be little remaining of the site that *could* remind. He had spoken often of the bombings, the pounding by British and American planes, night and day. And following liberation, the Russians had looted the complex. How much was repaired and how much rebuilt? Would he recognize the place?

The trams out to the island took an hour, and as my father failed to catch the attention of anyone else, he was treated to more of my value-added spiel, where I unloaded the facts he may or may not have known as I tried hard not to sound like a precocious child.

"Dad, did you know that Csepel is the biggest island in the Danube but not the biggest island in Budapest?"

He thought about that for a few seconds. "Now that you say, yes, I think. Most of the island is not in Budapest. Right?"

"Correct, advance to the lightning round. Baron Manfred Weiss, the guy who founded it all—Jew or not a Jew?"

My father hadn't been born Hungarian, of course, nor had he been long in Budapest. His time in Csepel had been spent getting by as best he could in dangerous and deteriorating conditions. He would have had little reason to be interested in the history—the ironies—surrounding the place, which had been founded by the Jewish industrialist Manfred Weiss, who had been created Baron de Csepel for his services. But Dad knew the general outlines. The vast war machine was the product of Jewish ingenuity and managed by assimilated Hungarian Jews. Also ironic: the Nazis insisted on buying the factories from the imprisoned family in 1944, sending them to Portugal even as they were slaughtering Jews elsewhere.

My father didn't know it at the time, but he had shared the island with prominent Jewish cultural figures, businesspeople, writers, journalists, and intellectuals housed not far from him, near prime spots for bombing. The Hungarians used Jews as human shields, and if that didn't work, the bombing was a handy method of removing them—friendly fire, in a way. More irony. Part of the point of collecting these prominent Jews was to humiliate them. They were gathered together under a simple single classification. My father was the poorest of the poor and from observant, even Hasidic, stock. The Weisses were industrialists, underwriters of war, with—besides their factories—a valuable art collection to plunder that remains the subject of lawsuits. The Germans and their Hungarian allies had united very disparate sorts in ghetto and camp and death. Imre, elegant and university educated, and my father were good examples. My father's early poverty, the frequent missed meals and grinding physical labor, advantaged him over Imre and others. The miserable food and hard labor were familiar. The beatings too, for that matter.

Several minutes' walk brought us to a pillared gate, with an exceedingly worn sign telling us we were at Csepel. It was quiet, though not ghost-town silent, with faint percussive and grinding sounds in the distance.

"Is this the entrance from then, the one you went out of? Right here?"

"This is it. Different, of course. Not this sign. This is from the communists, I think. But over that way they had the trucks that took the workers to the different stations for getting to the city and other places."

Yards from where we stood, Imre had preceded him, never looked back, mounted a truck. Dad had been forced to run furiously after it, had nearly missed it. Was I missing something in the account—which I had heard many times? Was my father missing something?

He had halted, just gazing up at the sign and at the wall for what seemed a long time.

"Hey, Dad, there's nobody out here. Let's go in."

I meant no one was around to stop us.

"It was steel on top over the gate—had a gate with bars. Well, we go."

And he led us in. As we moved down a narrow street, there was an immediate sense of enclosure. Glimpsed through gaps, tall chimneys pointed skyward in the distance. The space around us was caged in steel: above, a crisscross of girders and beams and a walkway or two. Multiple lines of pipes ran along and between the sides of buildings, and a forest of stanchions stood among stunted trees, weeds, and clumps of grass.

186

"You, know, Jason, there was only brown here and gray, what I noticed first about Csepel then."

It was easy to imagine this installation doubling as a forced-labor camp. I recorded something of the place, and my father in it. Even as I trained the lens around me, I thought that the structures in view, old as they appeared, must be aging reconstructions of what had been destroyed during the war. The grim gray serviceability of the buildings around, mostly large huts joined in rows, suggested that little of the original Manfred Weiss works remained. There was a mounting fricative drone from several cavernous openings—also the snap of arc welding and the high whine of some drilling. A few men inside paused their work to watch us pass.

"Dad, the street must be all changed. So much corrugated metal on the sides here—they aren't that old. Even the brick buildings, as bad as they look, must be well after your time here."

But he wasn't looking up at the buildings or in at the men. I'd expected him to take us into one of these work sheds to speak to people, but he was staring at the ground, at the large cobbles and embedded rails—if restored, they had been restored to exactly what they had been. They seemed artifacts from the beginning, of the whole factory, early twentieth century.

"No, here, I recognize," he said, pointing first to the rails and then farther ahead. "Right here we took things on these rails, loading the cars to the smelter. Here, remember I told you, was Gunga Din, we called him, who brought us water." His voice was quiet, a sort of wonder in the tone.

We walked on, twenty or thirty yards perhaps, when my father stopped in front of a square concrete box, upright slabs and a capstone of a roof with a cast-iron vent protruding, and an iron plate inset where the door would have been. Three or four similar structures rose out of long grass. He pointed at them.

"This was a bunker of sorts, Jason. Wonderful. This was a bunker. During the bombing, we were hiding. It wasn't a good protection. Just from shrapnel."

He walked over to one, exclaiming quietly, "My God." He swung his hand out, as if introducing someone. Was he inviting me to take some more video?

"What is it?" I asked him.

"This was an underground bunker...we lived in."

He sounded almost matter-of-fact. Did he just then remember? The first memory was the search for shelter from the bombing, then the recollection that these had provided another sort of shelter, such as it was. We moved together across the narrow road to a bunker entrance that had stairs, descending about ten feet to a door behind some metal mesh, with a sign on it.

"Dad, why don't you go down and take a closer look?"

"There's a warning. It's now some electricity."

"You could just take a look…"

"No, no, let's go."

We wandered off down the road, deeper into the complex, turning almost at random, inspecting various areas. I got no distinct sense that he'd been further reminded of much else by the site, but I followed along beside him. A gate blocked the way into one installation—an odd sign over it—a rusty arch of metal with the words in Spanish, *Establecimiento Metalurgico*. We backtracked and found another way to proceed to wherever we were going. We talked about keeping our bearings by a set of chimneys. As I took video of them, I couldn't help thinking of those other chimneys, the ones that conducted Jewish ash into the sky. My father had been here laboring for industry that supported that other industry, the death factory where he was intended to go.

"You know the worst job I had was putting back the electrical wires from the bombing. We were outside of Csepel. People died from fixing wires."

"Well, they weren't very careful with the Jews, were they?"

"Depended who you were with, who was in charge—some of them were real anti-Semites, others not so bad. You could be here doing one kind of work almost like a regular workman and over there might be hell. The scrap metal was dangerous but we had courage for each other. The wires, they rushed too much."

"But if you were outside the complex, wouldn't that have been the time to escape?"

"Maybe I could have, but where would I go? I had a plan with Imre, a place."

"Except there was no room for you in the end, where Imre was going to hide."

*My father in Csepel, near the spot where he and other Jews had loaded scrap to be melted for Axis war materials*

He looked at me, "Imre didn't know that. He said only there was a chance."

I didn't pursue the subject further. We ambled around some more—down near the Danube now. The river lay near the factories, the view blocked by buildings and scrub trees. When the bombers came, he had had to run for the mud near the riverbank, which would blunt the force of the blasts. Very close sometimes. Once, some shrapnel detached part of his nose, which a shoemaker repaired, the scar neatly following a natural line over the wing of his nostril. That was a story he seldom retold. I thought the nearly invisible scar was the thing—a vanity, but it could well have been the terror of the memory, and companions killed too. How could I know? They might vary, the reasons for telling or not. And I was often enough informed I was mistaken, when I ventured to say something aloud. Imre was a hero. Gunga Din was a hero, not simple-minded at all, tender to the others and admired by all of them.

With Imre as with other supporting characters in my father's saga, I was stuck with my native understanding of them, and of events. And by

189

my father's lights I got things wrong, very wrong, and sometimes didn't get it at all.

I could tell by the chimneys that we were not far from the entrance now. "Maybe we'll be able to see the river up there," I said, walking ahead.

"OK. But then we should get the tram, yes? I'm a little tired."

No water was in view; just a water tower and beside it a huge square cement structure, windowless, a couple of stories high. The surface was cracked and crumbling. It seemed old enough to have been here since the war.

"Dad, look at this thing. What is it?"

He looked for a few seconds, nodded, shrugged. "There were I don't know how many of these, new when I was here. That's *their* bunker, for the workers, it's down very deep. We weren't allowed in. I told you so many of the boys died from the bombing."

Soon we exited the gate to the road, where there was a tram stop close by, where more than fifty-five years ago Imre had run for a truck. Was that a natural thing to do, to leap on and to assume his coconspirator was right behind him? Wouldn't walking, an ordinary pace, be more like an ordinary departure? Though I guess people do run to catch the first bus, or truck in this instance. But still, he had nearly lost my father, who had raced frantically, barely made it. Dad said he knew where Imre lived, but he didn't seem sure of the place now, and he remembered other addresses—other places evidently hadn't changed so much, hadn't proved so elusive. On the one hand…on the other hand…I was out of hands. It simply occurred to me to wonder if Imre was not as attached to my father as my father was to Imre. Maybe that running ahead was just a subtle thing, and too little to go on. Such efforts at interpretation, only to get to a place of uncertainty. I would have to rest in uncertainty about my father's judgment of those he thought closest to him.

I could no more guess what was in Imre's mind than I could that of my uncle, Shmuel. It was impossible to get near either. And what should I think of my father's insistence that Imre was a pivotal character, without whose support he would not have survived? Without whose support I would not have existed? This whole trip, my whole life, there would be that element: trying to enter another's mind, the other, the native speaker from a different native place—the mind of my father and all those other others whose lives touched his in such significant ways, and therefore touched mine. That *therefore*! What I have understood since boyhood was that my father's story had everything to do with me. My very existence, yes, but beyond even that, it contained so much of value, Jewish history and my particular inheritance, both. In a Holocaust archive interview of my father, my mother was given a few minutes at the end of the tape. She put it grandly this way: his story was a symbol of the Jewish people, the story of the Jewish people, in their survival and eventual triumph. The statement made perfect sense to me. The stories represented my confirmation more than a bar mitzvah. And they had been given into my keeping, whatever I thought.

The stories kept testing my understanding in many ways, but particularly in the area of how to keep things of value. For, as this trip showed so many times, I wasn't always sure of the value each episode enshrined, despite my father's clear notions. Imre stood for the power of friendship with someone of noble character, worthy of admiration. Noble would be the sort of language he would use for Imre. Had it been Imre's idea to escape? No, they were equal companions in the risky venture. But Imre had shelter in town. Imre had organized a way to avoid the Germans and Hungarians and to await the approaching Russians. But there was no room for my dad. He was on his own.

Is that why, guilty at having failed my father, Imre did not find my father after the war? Guilt at having failed to feel for my dad quite what he had felt for him? Perhaps their feelings for each other, as about many things, didn't align. Here again I was processing events—or nonevents— around Imre in my own way, on insufficient evidence. I, who didn't feel about things as my father did. Who didn't feel for him as he wanted me to. And I was uncertain of what he felt for me; I didn't think he had much idea of what my interior was like. I thought I knew that I was a sort of possession, given in compensation for losses. I knew sometimes what he wanted of me as a special sort of audience, specially eager, absorptive. But our feelings often didn't align. I doubted Imre, and my father could tell. But hadn't I gone on this trip to find better alignment? He must have known that too.

NEW ROCHELLE

# Afterword

*He knows his father's resistance*

*to memory. His father has forgotten that beating*
*when his son, late, took the story from his hands,*
*joining it after the worst and without resistance.*

WRITING THIS BOOK HAS MADE ME FOCUS on the day and date of events, even in my own life. Though I believe the impulse is of long standing. Still, so much of my effort has been directed toward temporal and geographical exactness: when my young uncle was taken away on the train, when he came to the bridge, where that bridge was; trying to fix the stories on some sort of external grid, lines on the map, the boxes on a calendar.

No matter how precise their internal detail, survivors' narratives often float free of those markers that might help those who were not there, hadn't been born yet, or don't grasp the historical detail. I began to need, as I grew up around my survivors, some sense of where the things they told me fit into a whole. The figures in these stories—father, aunt, uncle—had seemed gargantuan, figures that filled my sky, but the world of the family necessarily diminished as more of the world itself was available to me. I could move around it more. I had a greater awareness of its past, learning, for example, that Jews had not just been despised from 1938 to 1945. That the Germans took direct control of Hungary, and Eichmann began the final solution for Hungarian Jews, in 1944, the year my father had been sent to the transit camp at Jolsva and from there to forced labor at the Csepel factory. The year my aunt Lilly and my uncle Shmuel went into the ghetto of Munkacs and from there were put on the transport to Auschwitz.

What had happened to my family was a fragment in a much larger mosaic, and even as I would always need to attend closely to their piece, I wanted to understand the rest. And placing the family accounting in a larger history began to feel like a contribution in itself—to them, yes, but even more so to me, to my own autonomy. I was adding something of value to what they had given me, using my skills, my mind, in helping to pass on a legacy placed in my hands. I felt I was exercising some measure of control, too, maybe correcting small inaccuracies in areas outside their immediate experience. Sometimes my insistence on finding the specifics of time and place or contemporaneous events felt like resistance, a countering by way of augmentation, to the overwhelming authority of their suffering. Permission, your honor, to cross-examine the witness.

For me and my cousins, when we were young, simply hearing of the intensity of the experiences of those who had survived was sufficient; it was a mark of intimacy to be told these things, especially by those who seldom spoke of them. But as time went on, the accounts were required by a world outside of family. The surrounding culture had taken notice in movies and television programs. Other people were interested, and in order to understand, they would need the details of the larger framework that the survivors didn't always have.

Even in personal circles of acquaintance my father had expanded his audience, more and more assuming the role of the survivor-witness. He took strangers into his confidence, until they didn't appear to be confidences anymore—nor the strangers, strangers, somehow, which made me increasingly, if vaguely, uncomfortable. When his teaching culminated in a public success as National Teacher of the Year, he began to have something of a career as a speaker—about the Holocaust as well as educational issues. It began to seem to me that he wanted something for the telling, that the more he claimed that his activities were obligations, performed for the greater good, a chastening, a warning, a contribution to "never again," the more they seemed to be ego-bound.

As a young man, I had a puritanical view of motivation, less tolerant than now of what I thought was lesser. I required the man who ran into the burning building to save the child to be entirely unaware of the cameras on him. For me, the true hero's reflex needed to be at work—the impulse that is overwhelming and entirely sincere because practically autonomic, unavailable for conscious modification. I grew less insistent on such purity, dubious that it was even possible and of course eager to have my own failures at attaining utter nobility of purpose forgiven. I sought permission to be a witness myself, permission to plead the Fifth Amendment when necessary.

Among the facts in evidence: my father had been made to feel he was worth less than nothing, and not by gentiles alone. However, it was by gentiles and because he was Jewish that a plan was put in place to murder him. Because he was a Jew, he could be rounded up and put to forced labor, betrayed to Germans; he could expect the official machinery of the state of which he was citizen to hand him over to be murdered. If anything could be restored to him by his speaking, let him have it. It's little enough.

What would I like for my telling? My own satisfaction that I have managed to relate as much of the truth as anyone could say—or have. And, as with our trip together, I would have liked my writing to have cleared a path between my father and me, so we could have had a fuller knowledge of each other, and a fuller acceptance and love. The knowledge is no longer possible, though fuller acceptance and love may be. I am fortunate in living long enough to identify my own need, though that much life also teaches that often to arrive at the knowledge of a need is to understand precisely what one is likely not to receive.

One barrier to a clear connection to my father has been an incident from my childhood, for which approximations of day and date have never seemed sufficient. I first set it down years ago in a poem titled "Joining the Story." The point of view of the piece is mid-distant third person—objective, omniscient—further distanced by a highly artificial verse form, a sestina: thirty-nine lines with a permuted set of words in lieu of rhyme. The repeated words are *resistance, memory, time, hands, join, story*. The narrative concerns a beating a child receives in the street when he was very late returning home. When the boy finally appears, his father, who had certainly been terrified that something awful had happened to his son, descends on him with a belt. The matter-of-fact, omniscient voice of the narrator reports the child's bewilderment and is also aware of details of the father's experiences in a way the stunned child is not. In time, the son will learn of the father's labor-camp beatings, one beating especially. The poem, rendered this way, allows for a certain deniability: it reads like a fiction. So neither my father nor I would necessarily have to acknowledge the content. In the poem is *the* father and *the* child; not *my* father, or *me*.

But it was me. I was beaten. Whatever the time of year, the weather was mild, and the day long enough and light enough to be summer. I was late coming home, down Harrison Avenue. I had been with friends, farther afield than usual, and I was young enough to lose track of time (seven, perhaps a little younger); to have been altogether unconscious of it for long periods; to sink utterly into what I was doing. But it was getting dark, and I headed home.

I don't recall seeing my father run toward me or being frightened. I think now that he must have been afraid, he converged on me with such suddenness. The sting of his belt seemed simultaneous with his arrival, and I don't remember saying anything or having a chance to. I don't know what I would have said.

I didn't yet understand about his beatings. As for mine, it was as if I were tumbling, catching glimpses of others at a pause in each turning—people on the stoops, walking the streets, a girl leaning against the bowed-out safety bars of a second-story window. Windows were open all around, a radio was playing, and there were the scuffing sounds of my father's footsteps as he swung at me. He was saying some things, I thought, in that way that speech is parceled out in the midst of such an activity. I don't think he was speaking English. And then there were the sounds of effort, grunt and puff. His own father had beaten him at a younger age than I was then, I believe, though those early beatings, delivered by his father, weren't what would make mine so insignificant.

I must have tried to dodge him, and he kept repositioning—that was when I heard the sound of his shoes against the grit of the street and when I had different views of objects in flashes: the black curbstone against the gray sidewalk, a waffle-checked manhole cover. I can't imagine that it lasted more than a few minutes, but I had no sense of how much time elapsed. Whatever it felt like then in the midst of whatever duration, I don't think of the incident in terror. I see now that my father's terror, and the anger it produced, came from imagining further loss: the loss of me, which in one sense was exactly what was happening, though not in the way he feared.

I wasn't aware of his losses then. I would hear about them soon after, beginning obliquely with the early, loving mention of his mother and the silence about his father. His family had been desperately poor and hungry much of the time. The comforts of my childhood—the ample food, the yeshiva education, the opportunity simply to play—all stood in quiet juxtaposition to what had been withheld from him. My privileges received explicit mention from time to time in classic fashion: when I wasn't eating what had been prepared, when I didn't seem grateful for what I had received. But the pointed instruction impressed less than what I gathered as I watched. Bones were picked clean and left in marrow-sucked splinters when he ate chicken or lamb chops.

Another beating stood between me and my father when I wanted to talk to him, even as an adult, about what had happened between us. That was the beating he suffered in Jolsva. When I tried to talk about my beating at his hands; when I wanted to know what he remembered of my beating (day and date, if I could have it) and whether that had been the first time; above all, when I wanted to raise the incident with him and explain how hard it had been afterward to believe him, to believe *in* him; when I needed to explain some things about the way I had been with him—the terrible scale of what had been done to him, to those he loved, made that time in the street feel minuscule. I could neither mention nor move past my own beating.

In the Jolsva incident, he hadn't quite struck the man but pushed him away from what he was doing to Dad's food—fouling it, as he passed; spitting in it, I think. And it wasn't only the food. The man was about my father's age, in uniform, a village bully like the ones he knew from Kustanovice who threw stones at Jewish children. My father had pushed him hard enough for it to be considered a blow. The soldier had him beaten by a group. And it had always been enough for me that he hadn't assented to what was done to him. It had always made sense that my dad, who seemed massive to me in anger, had resisted. He was in reality a small man, small enough to pass for younger than he was, a great advantage to his survival back then.

What had he exaggerated? What had I gotten wrong? He was always saying others had it worse, but what did that mean exactly, to him, short of dying? For sure, others must have had it better and taken it worse, or vice versa. He said that his poverty had advantaged him in labor camp—others couldn't live on the thin soup, but he had often half starved in the ordinary course of an impoverished childhood.

There is in the business of memory inevitable approximation, conscious and unconscious, and the recognition of that is hard for me for some reason. I fear it. In my father I fear it may distort some crucial matter—in his witness, in the record of what happened to the Jews. I am also afraid that I may add to some misperception by misremembering what my survivor father said. I want to have his report, and my report of his, perfectly true. I know intellectually that this is some sort of fantasy, and that in human memory as in other human things there is no perfection. And what is that anyway and who is to judge? (Me. At twelve, at twenty, at thirty-five, at fifty-one.)

Any time my father got something wrong in our ordinary lives, as people do, some minor matter (that he might yet insist about, sure he was right) such as where the car had been left in a lot, I wondered what he'd gotten wrong in his testimony. For that's what it was. If he had gotten some little thing wrong, could he have been mistaken, or worse, on larger matters? We had all made way for his memories—bore with them, bore up under them. It mattered deeply to me that whatever we had sacrificed, my mother and I, was sacrificed for what was true.

I made very little space for differences in individual perception and temperament in my ideal of survivor narration. There must be above all no posturing, no self-aggrandizement. No exaggeration, no stoicism or philosophizing in other forms. For God's sake no paradoxes, which had to be dead ends: was anticipation really the worst? Could it be the lash about to fall rather than the burn of the falling lash? Still, what could he have said, and what manner of saying would not have invited minute examination from me? Though for most of my life, these were the questions I'd kept to myself. Permission to approach; permission to treat the witness as a stranger.

I once saw formal questioning of a witness, a Polish man named Jablonski, in a videotaped deposition for a Holocaust trial at the Justice Department's Office of Special Investigations. David Marwell showed me the tape when I visited him there in the early eighties, and it impressed me deeply. The accused, Bohdan Koziy, had been a Ukrainian auxiliary policeman and an enthusiastic collaborator with the Germans during the war. Jablonski's deposition was part of the work David and his colleagues at Special Investigations had done for the trial, which aimed at stripping Koziy of American citizenship and deporting him to where he might be tried for war crimes.

Jablonski sat in a nondescript meeting room, and the rhythms of communication were odd because of the delay for consecutive translation, every utterance of the American prosecutor doubled in Polish. Jablonski had witnessed Koziy's shooting of a young Jewish girl. His responses were very general. He didn't seem to be trying to conceal or mitigate, but in recounting events of four decades before, he was minimally expressive and undetailed. Slowly, the American interrogator pressed him—about the girl, a child of four; about where he had been standing; and whether his view had been impeded. The questions, as they mounted, seemed to take on a crisper or more amplified tone, as if to get it through the muting of the translator. But there was some audible dissatisfaction communicated to Jablonski in that tone, even doubt about him as a witness. How far away was he? Did he really have a clear view? Was the child, Monica Singer, saying anything? Jablonski said that she had been pleading for her life.

As the questions increased in intensity, it became apparent that the interrogator was working on the witness, who tensed and tensed again, shifting in his chair. This was a friendly witness, wasn't he? Yet he was made to squirm. More pressure came—this time about the distance between Koziy and Monica, between the gun and the child's body, until finally Jablonski said in an outburst that Monica was no distance from Koziy at all, that "he was holding her hand." He may have even said that twice, looking as if he would rise from the chair.

I understood that forcing the drama was designed to elicit a more complete truth from the witness, the truth of what he felt, to draw him closer to the moments of his witnessing. Pressing him made for persuasive testimony for those who would judge, in addition to reviving more specific recollection. But outside of such stressors as sworn testimony, such drama might be used for less noble purposes, perhaps not counterfeited but shaped to an audience. What seemed imperative to me is that nothing be crafted for performance by someone who had told the story too many times, had seen what was effective in his telling. Apparently I have confidence that I, and many others besides, can discern the genuine.

Though I have often thought of that scene since the trip with my father, I can't say it was on my mind as we planned to go. I had no conscious desire to assay or magnify the emotion of my father's testimony in any way. But I suppose it was there in me somewhere, that I expected his narrative might change on that old home ground, with all those reminders. But I avoided the specifics of what that might mean. Was it rawness I wanted to see? About Shmuel I can remember both of us using the phrase "honoring his memory," which sounds properly ceremonial. But for me that was a screen behind which must have been my sense that something might be ripped open in the neat fabric of his stories, and that I would love him more for seeing that. Besides, at the heart of the trip was a search for details not in his possession, the reality of a place he hadn't been: the place where Shmuel had died. For a change, he would be waiting for part of a story right along with me, having to find a way to imagine it. We would be equals in that respect, in a way we rarely, if ever, were.

And now, twenty years after that trip, there is no question of his accuracy as a witness. That is gone—well, comes and goes. He has days of remarkable lucidity, but sometimes familiar stories get utterly garbled. He misunderstands questions: either he doesn't hear properly or, as becomes increasingly apparent, has difficulty processing what he does hear. Years ago, when he was eighty-eight, ten years after our journey together, he gave an interview to a Holocaust archive in Westchester, which I discovered lately online. He reported his own life incorrectly. I winced my way through his responses to questions and saw that the questioners, a group of teachers, were alerted by the occasional non sequitur that he was offtrack. But they couldn't have possibly known how offtrack he was. At one point he assigned to his brother his own escape from labor camp—and added in the immediate aftermath of the war a journey back to Munkacs that never happened. Though horrified, I still admired the way he made them laugh, distracted, maneuvered, recovered himself. If he couldn't find the thread, he made a new one. This occurred during a period when he was taking care of my mother, who was almost entirely submerged in dementia. His interviewers couldn't possibly have appreciated the extent of the survivor skills they were witnessing.

I listened to every segment of those recordings with a growing sense that despite all that was beyond him now—the sequence of his own life events, never mind the larger context that I had tried to be of service with: the dates, the places—he was making every effort to be truthful about what had happened. It was only himself that he misrepresented. He pretended he could understand and remember, just as he always pretended when he *could* understand and did have a reliable memory. He was trying very hard to maintain the sound he always made in every language that he spoke. The recordings captured the public person: the teacher, the wise and sensitive man concerned with the brotherhood of humankind, in which he believed, despite being a victim of its lapses. Here was the man in whom I did not believe. Do not believe.

Or at least that *was* the man. In the years since, it became clearer and clearer that his care was my responsibility, obviously and acutely so after the death of my mother, when the requirements of her caregiving disappeared. He had risen to those requirements despite what was happening to him. He resisted; he denied his faltering. He kept trying to move ahead as he had his whole life long, no matter what was ranged against him. But something that began between us somewhere along the way in Eastern Europe was suddenly completed. We had been in search of a bridge, an actual one, in the world, and—why had I not thought of this, the *bridges?*—another between us. He permitted my help at last, admitted he needed it in doing so much he could not do: clearing out and selling a house he could no longer afford, moving him into an apartment across from his synagogue, arranging for his home attendant.

With my wife, Allison, and son Gabriel, I come to see my dad in person, just before the pandemic. The first morning of our visit, we head to his apartment from a nearby bed-and-breakfast. My high school pal Jules is due to come over, and the forecast is for laughter. My father often asks after Jules and always welcomes his visits, saying that no one had changed less over the years. And it is true. Animated, warm, responsible, and steady, Jules had a long, expert career in human resources, and maintains a wonderfully intact streak of goofy.

No sooner are we through the door than Gabriel drags us directly to the living room fish tank, demanding to feed them as we promised he could. My dad's caregiver, Naana, has a huge brunch laid out in the dinette, beautifully arranged, the core of Ghanaian hospitality and maternal caring on par with the Jewish version. My father, who's forgotten he's already eaten, drifts to the table to eat again, which suits Naana.

She says, "Come, you sit here, cool dude."

Dad has taken to referring to himself this way, proudly retaining the phrase from a long-ago student's compliment. He says it as if it were current slang—and his students then certainly understood he had little idea of what was current but still thought of him warmly, as a cool dude indeed. The times I sat in on his classes, I saw the students' amusement at his efforts at American slang in his foreign accent, and I also saw their affection.

Rushing in from the fish, Gabriel intercepts his grandfather with the news that we are thinking about getting a pet—which we have barely discussed.

Dad says, "Oh, Gabriel, your father used to bring home animals."

My son turns to me accusingly, poised to charge me with a kind of hypocrisy—avoiding pets for him now when I had had them.

"But we couldn't keep them, Gabriel, the cats. They weren't allowed in the building where we lived then," I say.

"Pigeons, you had those pigeons," Dad says with a smile.

"No, Dad, I brought home cats. Your brother…it was Shmuel who kept pigeons."

We sit around the table and eat and Jules arrives. Never without his music, or his enthusiasms, he treats us to a current favorite from his cell phone, Keb' Mo's "A Better Man." My father pushes back his chair and is up and out into the open space behind, dancing. He moves economically, hands close to his sides, head a little down, his mouth set, lips a little protruding. In fact, it's the picture of "cool"—I have been told that the arms widely flung out would be a mark of the dork. Can he be aware of this? Or the rock-and-roll expression? He works a shuffle to the left; he works back to the right. He retreats. He advances. No old-man's shuffle, a dancer's. Gabriel flees the room. It is way too much for him, the song, his old grandpa's launch into steps. And the cheering that Jules and I do, for Dad's joy—the joy of the body back with him for a historyless moment, I want to call it that. Jules whoops more, and I find myself saying over and over again, "Yes, Dad, go, you're so good, so good." And I think that this perfectly contained but unreserved dance of my father's, this too was in my keeping, and I will remember it as long as I can remember anything: the dance and how I feel for the dancer.

# Epigraph Sources

THE EXTRACTS that preface each chapter in *Shmuel's Bridge* are from poems of mine published in the following volumes:

*Lifting the Stone*. London: Forest Books, 1991.

*Other People's Troubles*. Chicago: University of Chicago Press, 1997.

*The Man Who Sleeps in My Office*. Chicago: University of Chicago Press, 2004.

*The Laughter of Adam and Eve*. Carbondale: Southern Illinois University Press, 2013.

Preface: "The Property of the World," *Other People's Troubles*

Chapter 1: "Elegy," *The Man Who Sleeps in My Office*

Chapter 2: "The Property of the World," *Other People's Troubles*

Chapter 3: "Taking My Name," Section I, "Mengele Shitting," *Other People's Troubles*

Chapter 4: "Speaking of the Lost," Section III, "Mengele Shitting," *Other People's Troubles*

Chapter 5: "Saint Kevin, Blackbird, and Others," *The Laughter of Adam and Eve*

Chapter 6: "Lifting the Stone," *Lifting the Stone*, reprinted in *Other People's Troubles*

Chapter 7: "Meyer Tsits and the Children," *Lifting the Stone*, reprinted in *Other People's Troubles*

Chapter 8: "Speaking of the Lost," Section III, "Mengele Shitting," *Other People's Troubles*

Chapter 9: "Speaking of the Lost," Section III, "Mengele Shitting," *Other People's Troubles*

Chapter 10: "Lilly, Reparations," Section IV, "Mengele Shitting," *Other People's Troubles*

Chapter 11: "The One Who Knows All Language," *The Laughter of Adam and Eve*

Chapter 12: "Saint Kevin, Blackbird, and Others," *The Laughter of Adam and Eve*

Afterword: "Joining the Story," *Lifting the Stone*, reprinted in *Other People's Troubles*

# Author Bio

FROM A FAMILY OF REFUGEES AND SURVIVORS—of pogrom and Holocaust—Jason Sommer has been drawn to story, in his poems and now in prose. He is the author of five poetry collections—most recently *Portulans*, from the University of Chicago Press. His poems have earned a number of honors, including an Anna Davidson Rosenberg Award for poems about the Jewish experience and a reading at the program "Speech and Silence: Poetry and the Holocaust" at the National Holocaust Memorial Museum. He has held a Stegner Fellowship at Stanford University and has been recognized with a Whiting Foundation Writing Award.

His seven-year residence in Ireland began an involvement in literary translation that led to published versions of contemporary Irish-language poems and has continued with collaborative work on Chinese fiction that has brought important voices into English for the first time. He lives with his wife, Allison Brock, and son Gabriel across from Tower Grove Park in St. Louis, Missouri.